DOMINIK SCHMITT

IRONISCH | IRONIC
IKONISCH | ICONIC

30 Jahre aktuelle Kunst
galerie thomas hühsam

STIFTUNG KUNSTFONDS

NEU
START
KULTUR

SONDERFÖRDERPROGRAMM 20/21 - Dieser Katalog und die Ausstellung »BALSAM«, 15.5. - 17.7.2021 in der Galerie Thomas Hühsam in Offenbach am Main, werden unterstützt von NEUSTART KULTUR, ein Förderungsprogramm der Bundesregierung zur Unterstützung von Medien und Kultur.

SPECIAL FUNDING PROGRAM 20/21 - This catalog and the exhibition »BALSAM,« 15.5. - 17.7.2021 in the Galerie Thomas Hühsam in Offenbach am Main, Germany, are supported by NEUSTART KULTUR, a funding program of the federal government to support media and culture.

KERBER ART

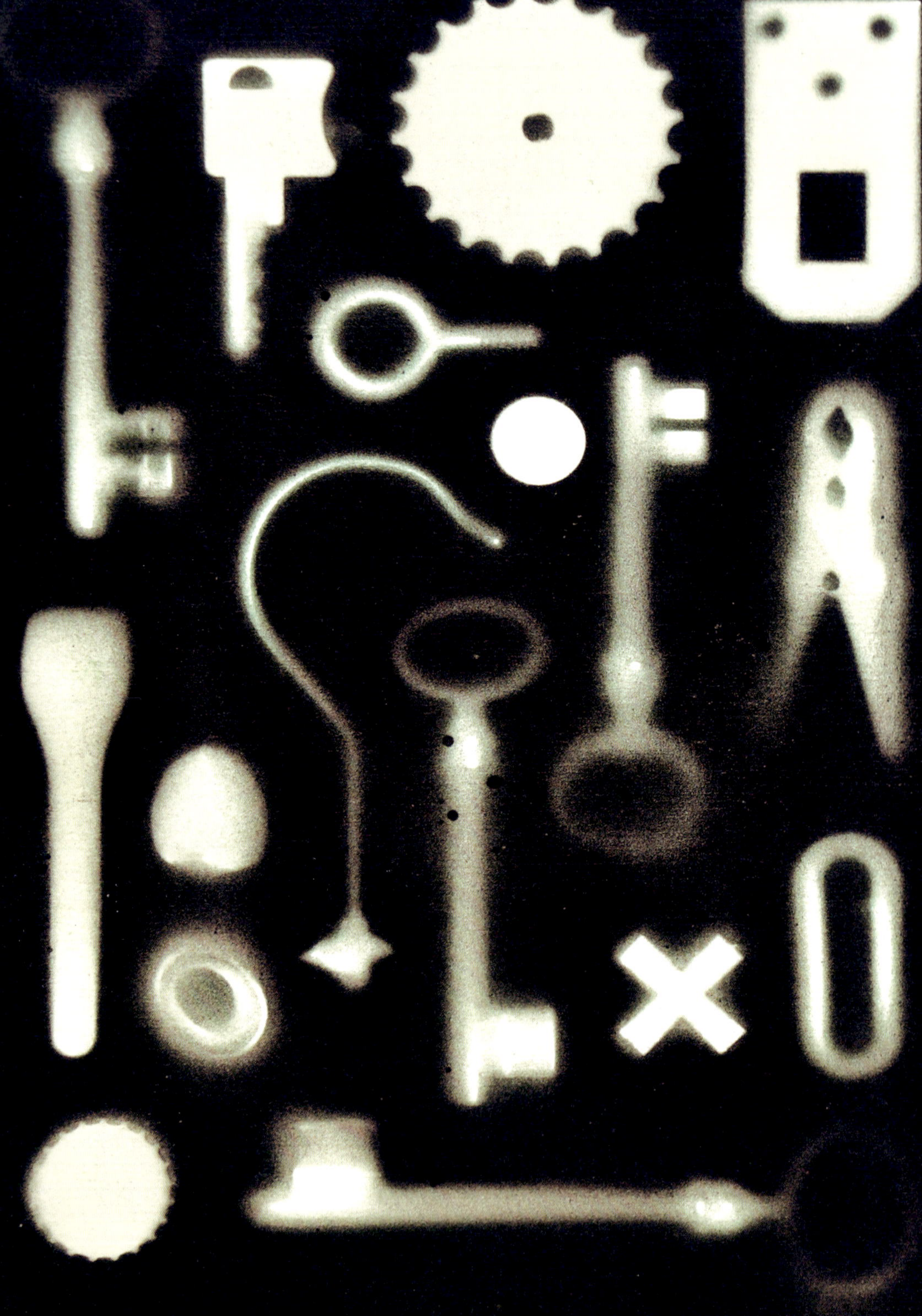

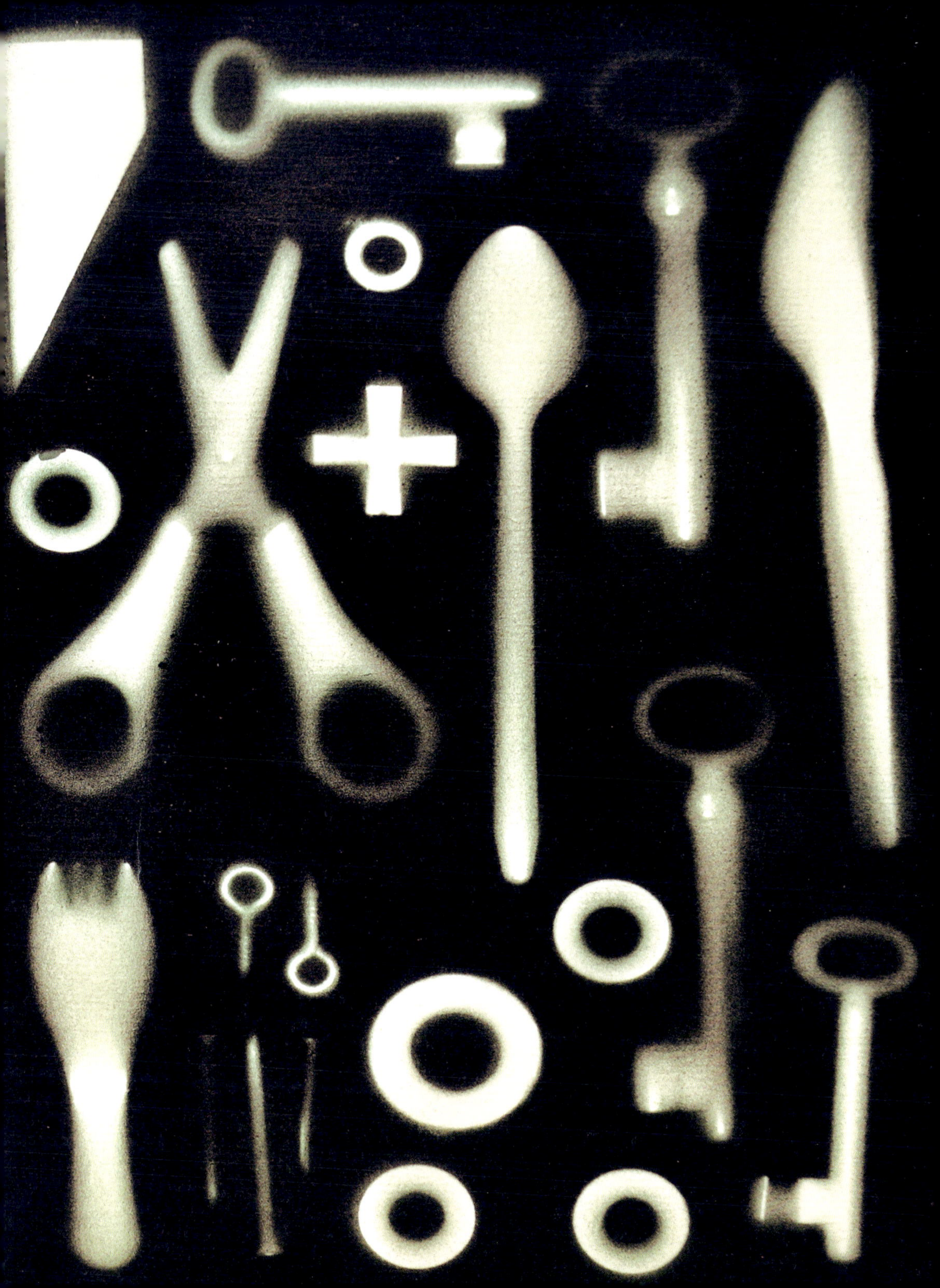

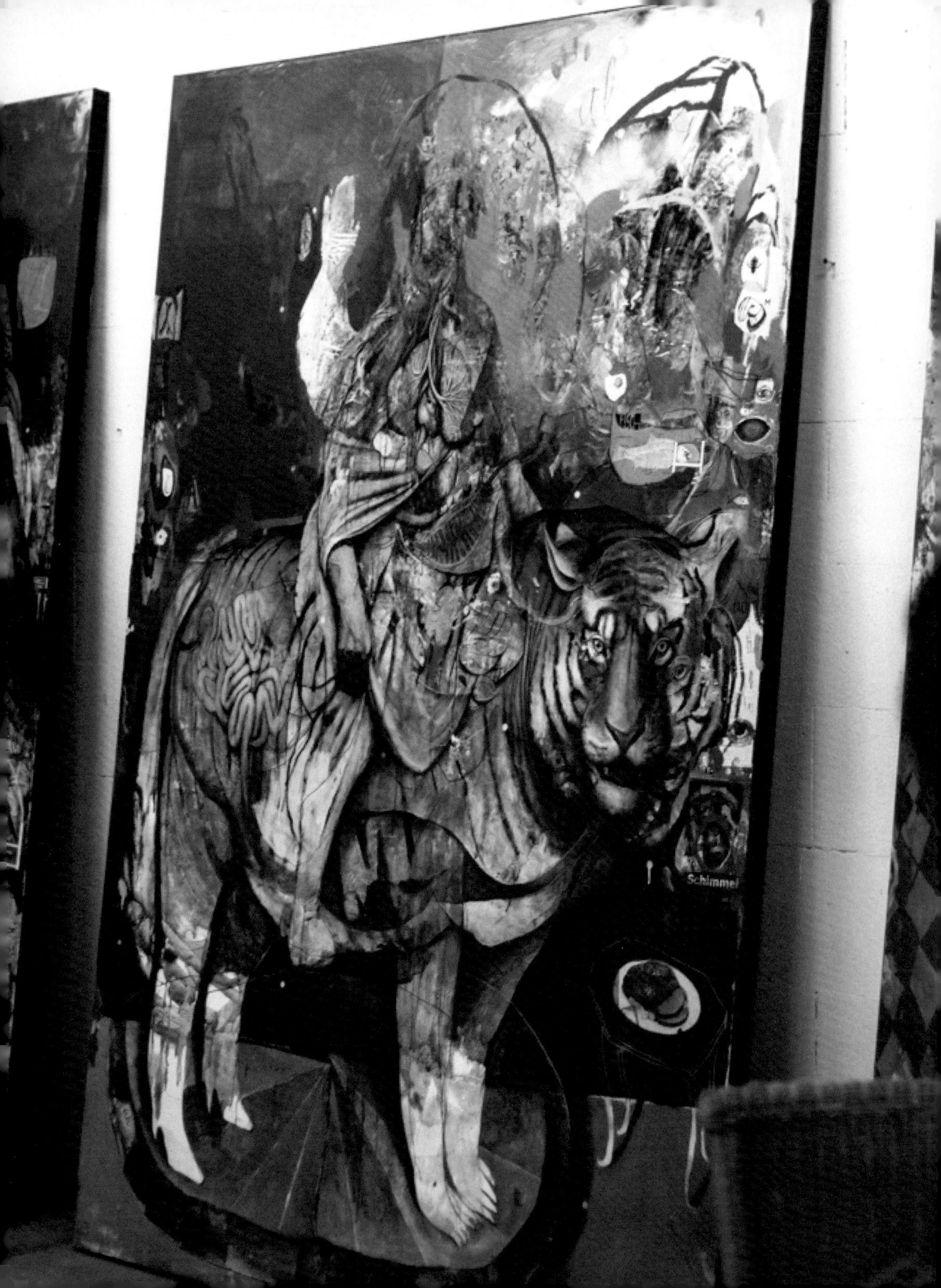
Schimmel

Vorwort | Foreword

Ingrid Walter, Journalistin und Autorin | Journalist and Author

»Thomas Hühsam war sofort begeistert von meinen Arbeiten und sah darin großes Potenzial. Er hat mich immer unterstützt. Inzwischen sind wir nicht nur Geschäftspartner, sondern auch Freunde.« So beschreibt Dominik Schmitt das Verhältnis zu seinem Galeristen in Offenbach am Main. In die Galerie Thomas Hühsam hatte ihn 2012 ein Sammler mitgenommen. Damals hing in den hohen hellen Räumen der ehemaligen Lederfabrik Ott gerade eine frischfreche Gruppenausstellung mit Werken des Pop-Art Künstlers Jim Avignon und anderen. Die offene und lockere Atmosphäre hat Dominik Schmitt gleich angesprochen. Vor allem begeisterte den eigenwilligen Künstler aber, dass Hühsam nicht nur ausstellt, was einfach und verkäuflich ist. Vielmehr zeigt und fördert er Positionen, von denen er persönlich überzeugt ist. So war der Grundstein für die gegenseitige Sympathie gelegt. Es dauerte nicht lange, bis Hühsam den damaligen Studenten im Atelier der Universität besuchte, wo er sich von dessen Arbeiten im Original überzeugte.

Sofort fühlte sich Thomas Hühsam von den faszinierenden Bildwelten Dominik Schmitts angezogen. »Die Ausdrucksweise von Dominik ist eigen und sehr stark. Ich sehe in der Kunst die absolute Freiheit der Selbsterfahrung und Dominik reizt das vom ersten Moment an kompromisslos aus«, sagt Thomas Hühsam. Schon bald ermöglichte er ihm die erste Teilnahme an einer Gruppenausstellung »Young Painters« (2013) in Offenbach am Main.

Geboren 1983, hat Dominik Schmitt an der Universität Koblenz-Landau am Campus Landau sein Studium 2015 mit dem Master für das gymnasiale Lehramt in den Fächern Biologie und Bildende Kunst abgeschlossen. Doch er haderte mit sich. In dieser Phase der Entscheidung malte er seine eigene Beerdigung. »(m)ein begräbnis in landau«, 2016, Mischtechnik

»Thomas Hühsam was immediately enthusiastic about my work and saw great potential in it. He has always supported me. Today, we are not only business partners, but also friends.« This is how Dominik Schmitt describes his relationship with the gallery owner in Offenbach am Main. A collector took him to the Thomas Hühsam Gallery in 2012. At the time, the bright, high-ceilinged rooms of the former Ott leather factory were hosting a fresh and cheeky group exhibition of works by Pop artist Jim Avignon and others. The open and relaxed atmosphere immediately appealed to Dominik Schmitt. Above all, however, the idiosyncratic artist was delighted that Hühsam does not only exhibit what is simple and easy to sell. Instead, the artistic positions he shows and promotes are in keeping with his personal convictions. Thus were the foundations laid for mutual sympathy. It was not long before Hühsam paid a visit to the then student in his studio at the university, wishing to see his work for himself in the original.

Thomas Hühsam was attracted at first sight by Dominik Schmitt's fascinating pictorial worlds. »Dominik's mode of expression is his own and very strong. I see in art the absolute freedom of self-experience and Dominik taps into this uncompromisingly from the very first moment,« says Thomas Hühsam. It was not long before he enabled the artist to take part for the first time in a group exhibition called "Young Painters" (2013) in Offenbach am Main.

Born in 1983, Dominik Schmitt graduated from the Landau campus of the University of Koblenz–Landau in 2015 with a master's degree, enabling him to teach biology and the visual arts at the Gymnasium. But he wrestled with himself. It was during this phase of decision-making that he painted his own funeral. »(m)ein begräbnis in Landau,« 2016, mixed media on canvas, (150 x 300 cm) is one of his most personal

auf Leinwand, (150 x 300 cm) ist eine seiner persönlichsten und wichtigsten Arbeiten. Es zeigt seinen möglichen Abschied von der Kunst, den er mit dem Eintritt in den Lehrberuf nahezu besiegelt sah – aber Dominik Schmitt mag keine halben Sachen. Ihm war klar, dass das Referendariat einen gravierenden Einschnitt in sein Kunstschaffen bedeuten würde. Auf dem Gemälde sind unter den Trauergästen Freund*innen, Familie und einige seiner wichtigsten Inspirationsquellen, Sammler*innen, Händler*innen und Galerist*innen, darunter auch Thomas Hühsam und sein Sohn Sikko Hühsam. Im Angesicht all dieser wichtigen Unterstützer*innen wurde Dominik Schmitt bewusst, dass der Lehrerberuf der falsche Weg wäre. Von da an konzentrierte er sich allein auf die Kunst.

»kausalkanon«, benannt nach seinem bisher größten Bild mit 2,50 x 4,80 m (Abb. S. 34 -35), ist die erste Einzelausstellung (Abb. S, 36 - 37), die Thomas Hühsam 2018 mit dem Künstler realisierte – eine bildgewaltige Schau, in der Dominik Schmitt bereits seine ganze Bandbreite an Inhalten und Techniken ausspielte. In seinen Werken blickt Dominik Schmitt immer wieder tief ins Innere eines jeden Menschen und fragt sich: »Was ist Wahrheit, wer bin ich und warum tue ich das, was ich tue?« Das Ich ist für ihn der einzige Filter durch den er selbst die Welt erfassen kann. »Auch, wenn meine Bildinhalte nicht immer für jeden leicht verdaulich sind, hat Thomas mich immer ermutigt weiterzumachen. Er erkannte meine Stärke, persönliche Gedanken so umzusetzen, dass es bei anderen etwas ausgelöst«, erklärt Schmitt, der nicht nur als Maler und Zeichner hervorgetreten ist, sondern auch mit filmischen Arbeiten, Skulpturen, früher auch mit Installationen, Musik und Lyrik.

Es entstanden weitere Kooperationen mit Galerien, Händlern und Verbindungen in die USA, in die Schweiz und nach Österreich. Erfolgreiche Gruppen- und Einzelausstellungen im In- und Ausland ließen nicht auf sich warten. Schmitts Arbeiten waren bereits im Pariser Grand Palais, im Wiener Palais Kinsky, im Istanbul Modern oder etwa der Berlinischen Galerie zu sehen. 2019 stellte er auf der Scope New York mit der Galerie

and important works. It shows his prospective farewell to art, a fate he saw all but sealed with his entry into the teaching profession. – But Dominik Schmitt doesn't like half-measures. It was clear to him that his teaching traineeship would bring about a serious break in his artistic career. Among the mourners in the painting are friends, family, and some of his most important sources of inspiration: collectors, dealers, and gallery owners – including Thomas Hühsam and his son Sikko. In the face of all these important supporters, Dominik Schmitt realized that the teaching profession would be the wrong path for him. From that moment on, he concentrated solely on art.

»Kausalkanon,« named after his largest painting to date, 250 x 480 cm (fig. p. 34 - 35), was the first solo exhibition (fig. p. 36 - 37) Thomas Hühsam realized with the artist. Staged in 2018, it was a visually powerful show in which Dominik Schmitt already displayed the broad range of his subject matter and techniques. In his works, Dominik Schmitt repeatedly looks deep inside each person and asks himself: »What is truth, who am I, and why do I do what I do?« For him, the self is the only filter through which he himself can grasp the world. »Even though the content of my imagery is not always easy for everyone to digest, Thomas has always encouraged me to keep going. He recognized my strength in translating personal thoughts in a way that provoked something in others,« explains Schmitt, who has emerged not only as a painter and draftsman, but also with video works, sculptures, and, before that, with installations, music, and verse.

Further collaborations with galleries and dealers came about, as well as ties to the U.S., Switzerland, and Austria. Successful group and solo exhibitions at home and abroad were also not long in coming. Schmitt's work has already been on view at such venues as Paris's Grand Palais, Vienna's Palais Kinsky, İstanbul Modern, and the Berlinische Galerie. In 2019, he exhibited at Scope New York with Miami's The Directed Art Modern gallery. He had his second solo exhibition at Thomas Huehsam's in 2020, entitled »status quo

The Directed Art Modern aus Miami aus. 2020 fand die zweite Einzelausstellung bei Thomas Hühsam mit dem Titel »status quo vadis in veritas ananas« (Abb. S. 88 - 89) statt. Inzwischen wird Dominik Schmitt international von Galerien in Österreich und den USA fest vertreten. In Deutschland haben ihn neben Thomas Hühsam in Offenbach am Main auch Galeristen in Hamburg und München unter Vertrag.

2020 – mitten in der Corona-Krise – wagte Dominik Schmitt, entgegen aller Trends in der Kunst, den Schritt zu Expansion. Er zog von seinem überschaubaren Gruppenatelier in Karlsruhe nach Landau in eine große, zweistöckige Halle. Hier hat er neben einem riesigen Arbeitsplatz auch eine großzügige Ausstellungsfläche, wodurch ihm die eigene Entwicklung immer vor Augen ist. Außerdem hat sich der Künstler dort einen multimedialen Arbeitsplatz eingerichtet, extra für seine Videokunst.

Nun freut er sich über die Ausstellung »BALSAM« (Abb. S. 132 - 133) in den Räumen der Galerie von Thomas Hühsam. Der Titel möchte aus dem Einerlei unserer Zeit herausleuchten und etwas Wohltuendes geben. »Die Menschen sollen mal durchatmen können«, sagt Schmitt und meint das auch für sich selbst. Doch zum Durchatmen bleibt dem aufstrebsamen Künstler nur bedingt Zeit. Die Nachfrage steigt stetig und Wartelisten für seine Werke werden immer länger. Einige Sammler*innen haben bereits zahlreiche Werke an ihren Wänden. Nun fehlt nur noch der Einzug in die museale Kunstwelt. Erste Anfragen gibt es bereits. Die Galerie Thomas Hühsam ist stolz darauf, den jungen Künstler Dominik Schmitt schon zu seinen Studienzeiten entdeckt zu haben. Der Galerist ist sich sicher »Dominik hat ein Ziel: Ganz nach oben kommen. Und ich weiß nicht, wer oder was ihn aufhalten sollte.«

vadis in veritas ananas« (fig. p. 88 - 89). Dominik Schmitt is now regularly represented internationally by galleries in Austria and the States. In Germany, alongside Thomas Hühsam in Offenbach am Main, gallery owners in Hamburg and Munich also have him under contract.

In 2020 – in the midst of the corona crisis and against all trends in art – Dominik Schmitt dared to expand. He moved from his medium-sized group studio in Karlsruhe to a large, two-story space in Landau. Here, in addition to a huge workspace, he also has a generous exhibition area, which allows him to keep a constant eye on his own development. In addition, the artist has set up a multimedia workspace there, specifically for his video art.

The artist is currently delighted with the exhibition »BALSAM« (fig. p. 132 -133) in the rooms of Thomas Hühsam's gallery. The title aims to stand out against the monotony of our times and offer something soothing. »People should be able to catch their breath,« says Schmitt, and he means that for himself as well. But the aspiring artist has in fact little time to do so. Demand is rising steadily, and waiting lists for his works continue to grow. Some collectors already have numerous of his works on their walls. The only thing missing now is the entry into the world of museum art, and here, initial inquiries have already been received. The Thomas Hühsam Gallery is proud to have discovered the young artist Dominik Schmitt back in his student days. The gallery owner is sure »Dominik has but one goal: to reach the top. And I don't know who or what should stop him from doing so.«

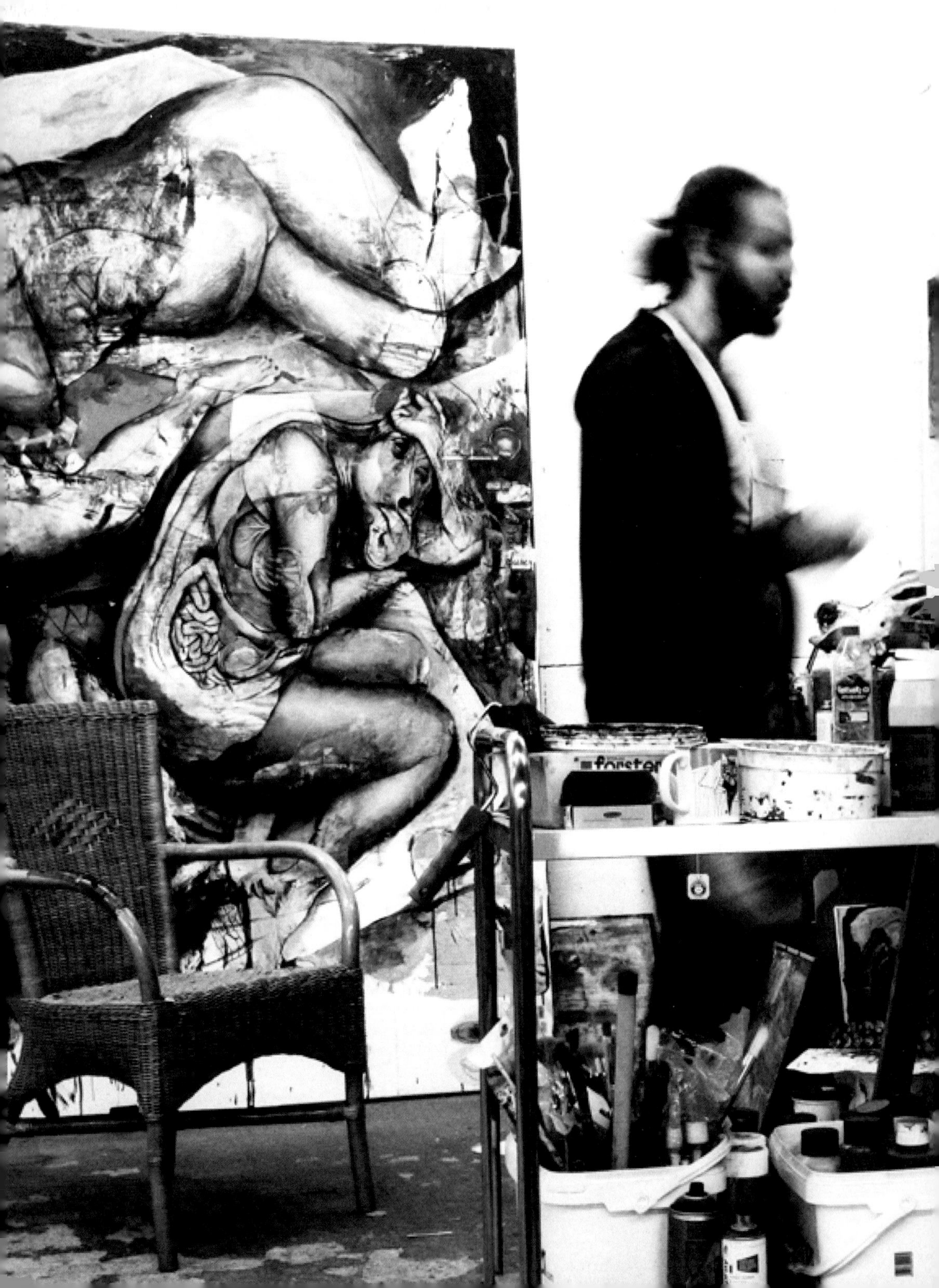

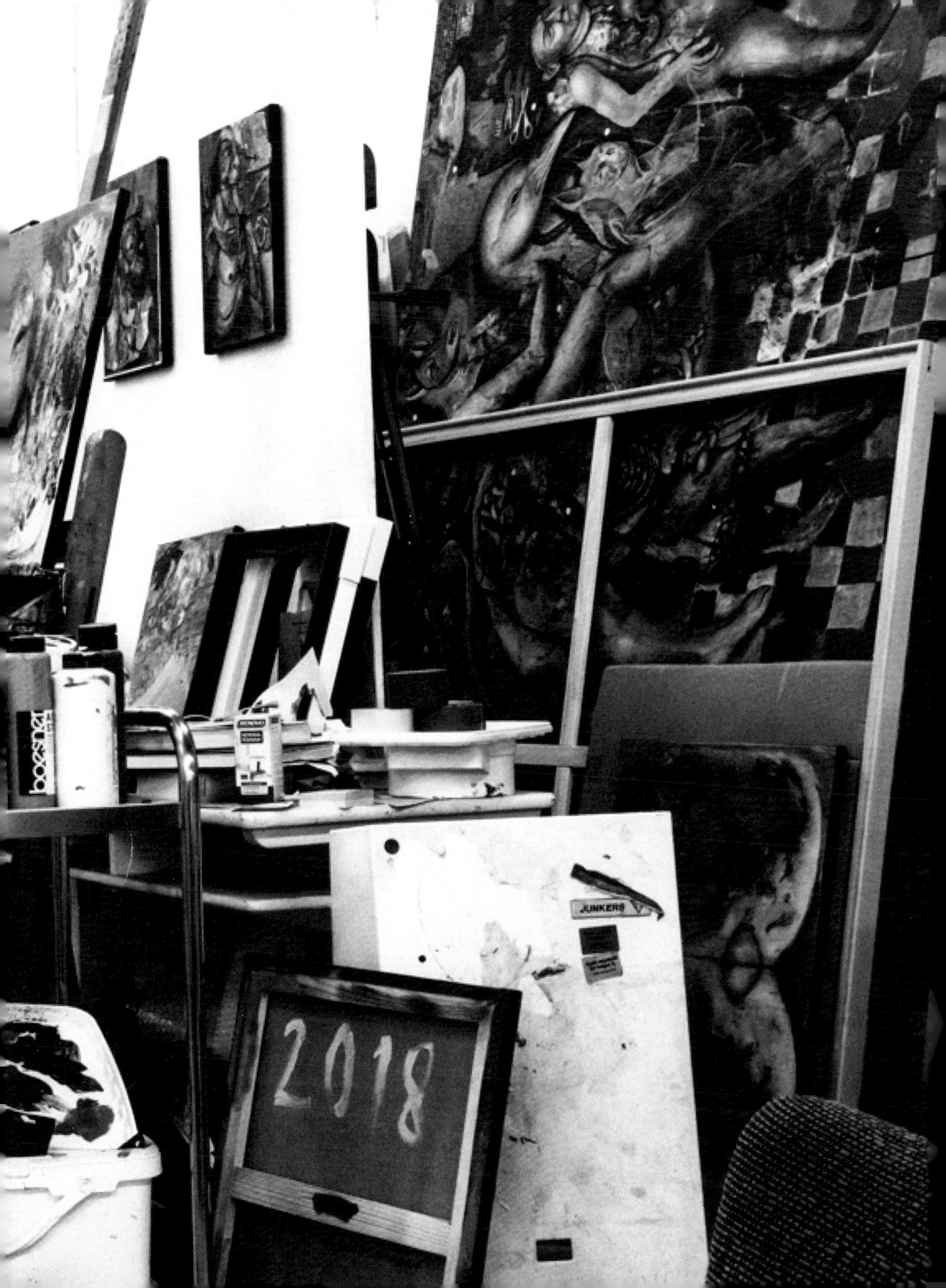
boesner
JUNKERS
2018

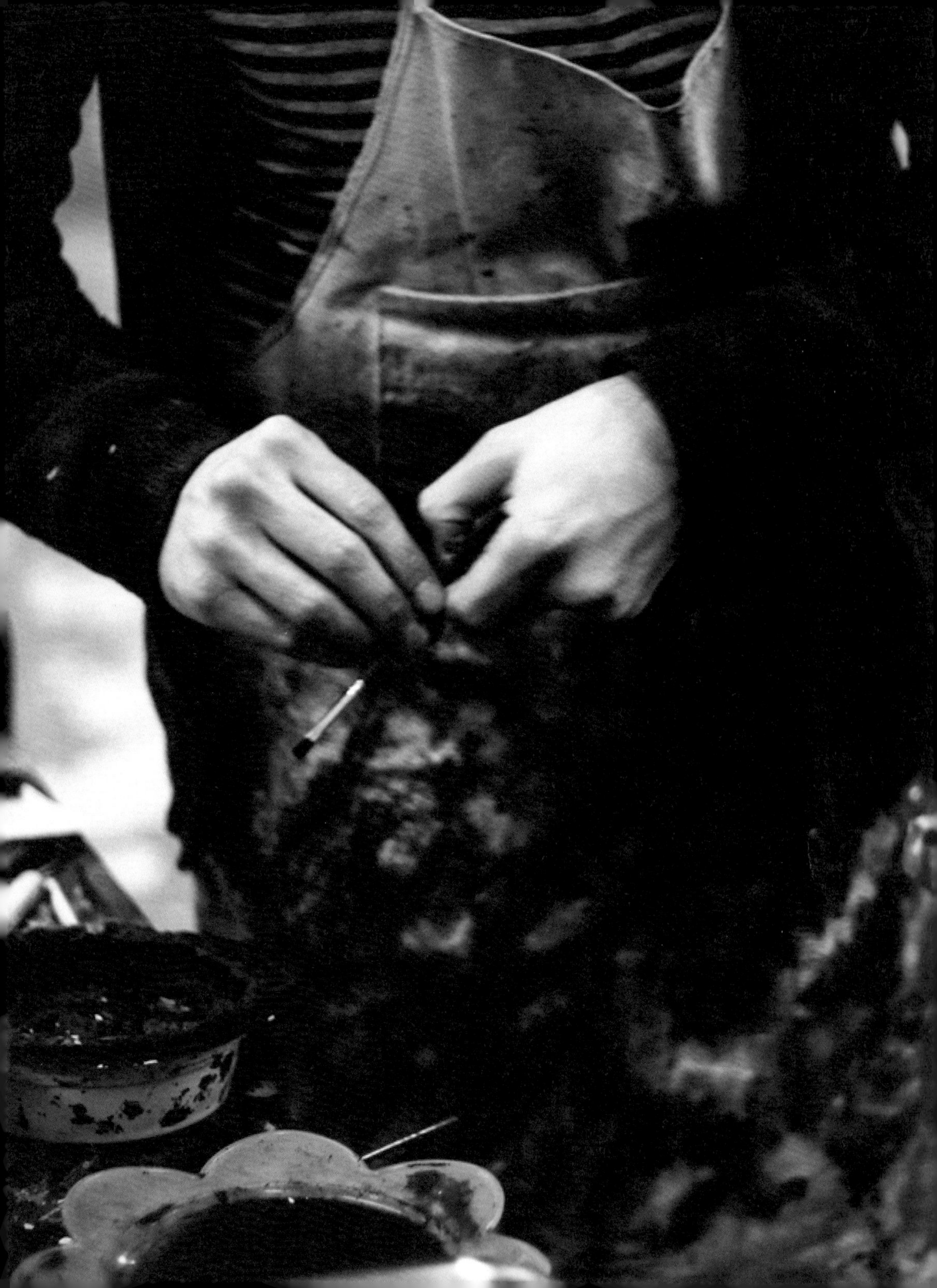

Ironisch Ikonisch | Ironic Iconic

Zur Kunst von Dominik Schmitt | On the work of Dominik Schmitt

Kristina Hoge, Galeristin, Kunstwissenschaftlerin, Dozentin | Gallery Director, Art Historian, Lecturer

Junge Kunstschaffende stehen heute angesichts der vergangenen Jahrhunderte Kunst und Kunstgeschichte und der überbordenden Vielfalt und Möglichkeiten des Kunstmarkts vor großen Herausforderungen: wie kann ich in diesem »Dschungel« meinen eigenen Weg finden, mich als Künstler behaupten und eine charakteristische, wiedererkennbare Handschrift entwickeln?

Dominik Schmitt ist dies zweifellos gelungen. Er schafft Bilder, die im besten Sinne eigenwillig sind, an denen der Blick hängen bleibt, die im Gedächtnis haften. Bilder, die die Betrachter*innen aufgrund ihrer Vielschichtigkeit und ihres Detailreichtums unmöglich auf den ersten Blick erfassen können. Sollten sie dies doch versuchen, so werden sie leicht getäuscht. Da ist zunächst die dunkle Farbigkeit mit einem reichen Spektrum an gebrochenen Schwarz-, Grau- und Erdtönen, die für eine irritierende, leicht melancholische Grundstimmung sorgt. Motivisch konfrontieren Schmitts Bilder mit dem Einblick in menschliches und tierisches Innenleben. Zwar dominiert das Figürliche, jedoch sind die Wesen in Schmitts Bildwelt immer höchst eigenwillige Existenzen aus einem Zwischenreich, angesiedelt jenseits der Realität. Immer wieder begegnen Amalgame von Mensch und Tier, oft mit deformierten oder disproportionalen Gliedmaßen, manchmal scheinen sie beinahe die Bildfläche zu sprengen – sie sind schrecklich schön und faszinieren in ihrer Einzigartigkeit, in ihrem Anderssein. Man fühlt sich vielleicht ein wenig hineinversetzt in die Figurenwelt von Kapitellen oder Wasserspeiern an romanischen und gotischen Kirchen oder die Höllendarstellungen eines Hieronymus Bosch oder Pieter Breughel – ein spielerischer Umgang mit Abgründigem und Erschreckendem.

Every young artist today faces great challenges in view of the past centuries of art and art history and the overwhelming diversity and possibilities found on the art market. How can I find my own way in this »jungle,« assert myself as an artist, and develop a characteristic and recognizable »handwriting«?

Dominik Schmitt has undoubtedly succeeded in this. He creates pictures that are idiosyncratic in the best sense of the word, that catch the eye, that linger in the memory. Pictures that the viewer cannot possibly grasp at first glance due to their complexity and richness of detail. Should he nonetheless try to do so, he will be easily deceived. First of all, there is the dark coloration with a rich spectrum of refracted black, gray, and earth tones, resulting in an unsettling and slightly melancholic basic mood. In terms of motifs, Schmitt's paintings confront us with glimpses into the inner workings of human and animal life. Although the figurative dominates, the creatures in Schmitt's pictorial world are always highly idiosyncratic beings from an in-between realm, located beyond reality. Again and again we encounter amalgams of human and animal, often with limbs deformed or out of proportion. They sometimes seem to almost jump out of the picture – possessing a terrible beauty and fascination in their uniqueness, in their otherness. One might feel a bit transported to the world of figures found on the capitals and among the gargoyles of Romanesque and Gothic churches, or in the depictions of hell of a Hieronymus Bosch or Pieter Breughel – a playful approach to the unfathomable and the frightening.

Hybrid creatures such as the »karlsruhe plate horse« (2019, fig. p. 67), the »stiletto goose« (2018, fig. p. 47), »the juice rabbit« (2019, fig. p. 63) or the »potato noodle dove« (2019, fig. p. 65) are simply fantastically absurd and provide their very own answers to the

Hybride Wesen wie das »karlsruher tellerpferd« (2019, Abb. S. 67), die »stöckelgans« (2018, Abb. S. 47), der »safthase« (2019, Abb. S. 63) oder die »schupfnudeltaube« (2019, Abb. S. 65) sind einfach fantastisch absurd und geben ganz eigene Antworten auf die Frage danach, was schön oder was richtig ist.

Die in den Bildern enthaltenen Schriftelemente – entweder in handschriftlichen Sequenzen oder als Collage fragmentarisch eingefügt – sowie oft auch schon die Titel der Arbeiten enthalten ironisch-witzige Brechungen und Wortspiele, die für den Gehalt und die empfundene Grundstimmung der Kompositionen immer von Bedeutung sind. So stellt Schmitt durch die Vielschichtigkeit seiner Bildelemente ebenso, wie durch die Doppeldeutigkeit oder dreiste Schwindelei seiner Titel – etwa wenn die Arbeit »der fette löwe« (2018, Abb. S. 53) doch so eindeutig einen Tiger zeigt – stets die Wahrnehmung und assoziativen Fähigkeiten der Betrachter*innen auf die Probe.

Je intensiver also die Auseinandersetzung mit der Bildwelt des Dominik Schmitt, desto weniger dunkel und düster erscheint sie. Stattdessen stecken die meisten Arbeiten voller scharfsinniger und humorvoller Anspielungen, nehmen Bezug auf die Kunstgeschichte, zitieren Vorbilder, reflektieren philosophische Inhalte und entfalten in ihrem Kreisen um das Mensch-Sein eine ganz eigene Poesie – ironisch ikonisch eben.

Keine Kunst, die sich leicht konsumieren lässt, sondern eine Kunst, die polarisiert und durch ihre Inhalte Diskussionen befördern möchte, etwa über Religion, den Lauf der Welt oder das Auflösen und Verschwimmen von Grenzen, zwischen Mensch und Tier, innen und außen, Traum und Wirklichkeit. Es ist eine Kunst, die nicht nur an der Oberfläche bleibt, sondern tief eindringt, in innere Schichten und doch gleichermaßen technische Raffinesse und ästhetische Aspekte impliziert.

Die Komplexität der Werke, die sich eben nicht auf den ersten Blick enthüllt, spiegelt sich auch in einer charakteristischen und vielschichtigen Arbeitstechnik, die Schmitt für sich entwickelt hat. In einem ersten Arbeitsschritt wird Papier auf Leinwand collagiert und

question of what is beautiful or what is right.

The written elements contained in the pictures – either in handwritten sequences or inserted fragmentarily as collage – and even the titles of the works themselves often contain ironic and witty inflections and puns. And they are always significant for the content and the perceived basic mood of the compositions. Thus, Schmitt always puts the viewer's perception and associative abilities to the test, and not only through the complexity of his pictorial elements. He also does so through the ambiguity or audacious deceitfulness of his titles – for example, when the work »the fat lion« (2018, fig. p. 53) so clearly shows a tiger.

Thus, the more intensively one examines the pictorial world of Dominik Schmitt, the less dark and gloomy it turns out to be. Instead, most of the works are full of astute and humorous allusions, making reference to art history, citing role models, reflecting on philosophical content, and unfolding their own unique poetry as they circle around what it means to be human – in a word, ironically iconic.

It is not an art that is easy to consume, but rather an art that polarizes and would like to generate discussion by means of its content: for example, about religion, the course of the world, or the dissolution and blurring of the lines between humans and animals, inside and out, dream and reality. It is an art that does not just dwell on the surface, but penetrates deep, into inner strata, while at the same time incorporating technical sophistication and aesthetic qualities.

The complexity of the works – which, at first glance, is easy to overlook – is also reflected in a characteristic and multi-layered working technique that Schmitt has developed for himself. In a first stage of work, paper is collaged on canvas and then provided with a layer of "muck" – consisting primarily of paste and other "additives." Only after this substrate is prepared does the actual pictorial arrangement follow on top of it. Especially in the current creative phase during the »corona pandemic,« there is another quite relevant and exciting preparatory step that should be mentioned. Following as it were in the footsteps of

dann mit einer Schicht »Dreck« – primär bestehend aus Kleister und weiteren »Zusätzen« – versehen, erst dann erfolgt auf den so präparierten Untergrund die eigentliche Bildanlage. Insbesondere in der aktuellen Schaffensphase während der »Corona-Pandemie«, ist hier noch ein durchaus relevanter und spannender Schritt als Vorarbeit zu erwähnen. Quasi auf den Spuren der sogenannten »Affichisten« des »Nouveau Réalisme« der 60er Jahre wandelnd, »sammelte« der Künstler Plakatabrisse etwa von Veranstaltungen, die nie stattgefunden haben. Dieser Technik der Décollage wohnt zunächst ein destruktiver, auflösender Prozess inne, der durch das collagierende Auftragen auf die Leinwand in sein Gegenteil gewandelt wird. Die Plakatfragmente werden zum eigentlichen Bildträger und ihre Titel oder Schriftsequenzen haben in der fertigen Arbeit häufig ein »Mitspracherecht«. So steht das Sehen und Sammeln dieser Informationen am Beginn der Bilder und stellt eine Art »Initialzündung«, einen Impuls dar, von dem ausgehend dann in einem »flow« die Arbeit direkt und intuitiv auf der Leinwand entwickelt wird.

Die Inspiration zu seiner speziellen Arbeitsweise erklärt Schmitt einerseits mit dem eigenen Anspruch trotz der eher zeichnerischen Prägung große Bilder machen zu wollen, was dazu führte, viele kleine Details zu einem großen Ganzen zusammenzufügen und auf der anderen Seite, habe der Boden des Ateliers, an dem festgeklebte und zufällig kombinierte Hinterlassenschaften ihre ganz eigene Schönheit entfalten, schon lange eine Faszination auf ihn ausgeübt.

Durch die spezifische Arbeitsweise mit ihren Schichten ergeben sich auf der Leinwand Überlagerungen, die manchmal beinahe haptische Qualität entfalten. Durch die gerissenen und aufcollagierten Plakatfragmente liegt den Arbeiten oftmals ein leicht nostalgisches Flair zugrunde, auch an den Charme bröckelnder Hauswände oder verblassenden Putzes wäre zu denken, so wie ja auch die Plakatschichten an die Vergänglichkeit und Kurzlebigkeit der Flut an Informationen, Veranstaltungen und Werbung erinnern. Verlaufende Farbspuren oder körnig grobe Partien,

the so-called affichistes of Nouveau Réalisme of the 1960s, the artist »collected« torn-off posters, such as of events that never took place. Initially, a destructive and disintegrative process is inherent in this technique of décollage, which is transformed into its opposite by the collage-like application to the canvas. The poster fragments become the actual medium of the image, and their titles or written sections often have a »say« in the finished work. Thus, seeing and collecting this information comes at the beginning of the pictures and represents a kind of »initial spark,« an impulse from which the work then »flows,« developing directly and intuitively onto the canvas.

Schmitt explains the inspiration for his special way of working, on the one hand, with his own aspiration to produce large pictures despite the more drawing-based character of his work, leading him to assemble many small details into a larger whole. On the other hand, he has long been fascinated by the floor of his studio, on which bits and pieces of past work are stuck and randomly combine to unfold their very own beauty.

The specific strata-based working method results in layerings on the canvas, which sometimes take on an almost haptic quality. Due to the torn and collaged poster fragments, the works often exude a slightly nostalgic flair, conjuring up the charm of crumbling house walls or fading plaster, just as the layers of posters remind us of the transience and ephemeral nature of the flood of information, events, and advertising. Progressive traces of color or grainy, coarse sections in which the background comes to the fore alternate with details finely executed to deceive the eye. Graphic elements appear next to or in monochrome areas of color, which, especially in more recent works, impart an increasingly airy quality to the overall composition.

The current work »sleeping cyclist« (2021, fig. p. 129) provides a particularly vivid example of this. Here, large areas right in the picture's foreground are simply left as colored surfaces and are set – tension-laden and with a circular movement – against a dense center.

Old master perfection is broken up by street-like

in denen der Untergrund zum Tragen kommt, wechseln mit augentäuscherisch fein ausgeführten Details. Grafische Elemente stehen neben oder in monochromen Farbflächen, die gerade in den neueren Arbeiten der Gesamtkomposition zunehmend mehr Luft verleihen.

Besonders anschaulich kommt dies etwa in der aktuellen Arbeit »schlafradler« (2021, Abb. S. 129) zum Ausdruck, in der direkt im Bildvordergrund große Bereiche nur als farbige Flächen stehen bleiben, gegen die spannungsreich das verdichtete Zentrum mit einer zirkulierenden Kreisbewegung gesetzt ist.

Altmeisterliche Perfektion wird gebrochen mit streetartiger Gegenwart. Die immer figurative Ausrichtung der Bilder wird doch auch ebenso bestimmt von arabesken Linienbündeln, Musterfragmenten oder freien zeichnerischen Kürzeln. Hell und Dunkel, schön und abstossend, schwarz-weiße Zurückgenommenheit und bunte Farbakzente, all diese Gegensatzpaare verleihen Schmitts Arbeiten das so charakteristische spannungsreiche Gesamtgefüge.

Das Zusammentragen aller in den Arbeiten enthaltenen Einzelelemente und Fragmente, appelliert immer an die kognitiven und visuellen Fähigkeiten des Betrachters, macht neugierig, die Puzzlestücke zusammenzutragen und wird deshalb nie langweilig.

Überhaupt ist in Schmitts Werk eine Vorliebe für das Spiel mit Überlagerungen festzustellen, auf die angesprochen der Künstler rein formal eine Beziehung zum Kubismus sowie ein dezidiertes Interesse an dem Aufzeigen von einem Davor-und-Dahinter bezeugt. Es sind unter anderem gerade diese charakteristisch verschachtelten, überlagerten Strukturen, die Betrachter*innen ganz hineinziehen in die Bilder und den Blick zum Ergründen der tieferen Ebenen einladen. Ein anschauliches Beispiel hierfür liefert der »nudelsiebtheoretiker« (2021, Abb. S. 131), dessen Arme den Bildgrund zu durchdringen scheinen, so wie im Gegensatz dazu die Flügel des »alten Falters« (2019, Abb. S. 78 - 79) optisch wie aufgefächert vor der planen Bildfläche stehen.

Technisch ist der Künstler überaus variantenreich.

presence. The always figurative orientation of the pictures is nevertheless also defined by arabesque line bundles, pattern fragments, or freely drawn abbreviations. Light and dark, beautiful and repulsive, black-and-white restraint and colorful accents, all these contrasting pairs give Schmitt's works their characteristically tension-laden overall structure.

The gathering together of all the individual elements and fragments contained in the works always appeals to the cognitive and visual abilities of the viewer, arousing their curiosity to put the pieces of the puzzle together and thus keeping the works from ever getting boring.

In Schmitt's work in general, there is a preference for playing with layering, to superimposing one element upon another. When asked about this, the artist refers, in purely formal terms, to a relationship to Cubism, as well as to a decided interest in pointing out an »in front of« and a »behind.« It is precisely these characteristically nested, layered structures that draw the viewer completely into the pictures and invite the eye to delve into deeper levels. A vivid example of this is provided by the »noodle colander theorist« (2021, fig. p. 131), whose arms seem to pierce the picture's surface, just as, in contrast, the wings of the »old moth« (2019, fig. p. 78 - 79) create the visual impression of being fanned out in front of the picture's flat surface.

In terms of technique, the artist commands an exceedingly rich variety. In addition to collage, drawing, and painting, we also encounter stencil and writing elements. Schmitt's work refuses to be categorized unambiguously, just as it refuses a one-sided stylistic classification. Elements evocative of the pictorial worlds of a Bosch or Breughel appear alongside stylistic borrowings from Cubism. Notions of Surrealism with its écriture automatique and tendency toward introversion are just as recognizable as elements of Street Art with its use of script, spray paint, and stencils.

Authenticity is a very important factor for Schmitt, and so there is always something of himself in all his pictures. This can be quite literally the case, as

Neben Collage, Zeichnung und Malerei begegnen auch Stencil- und Schriftelemente. Eindeutigen Kategorisierungen verweigert sich Schmitts Werk ebenso wie einer einseitigen stilistischen Zuordnung. Erinnerungen an die Bildwelten eines Bosch oder Breughel stehen neben stilistischen Anleihen am Kubismus. Gedanken des Surrealisums mit seiner écriture automatique und dem Hang zur Introversion sind ebenso erkennbar wie Elemente der Street Art mit dem Einsatz von Schrift, Spraypaint und Schablonen.

Authentizität ist für Schmitt ein ganz wichtiger Faktor und so steckt in allen seinen Bildern immer etwas von ihm selbst. Das kann ganz wörtlich aufgefasst zum Beispiel eines der häufigen Selbstbildnisse sein, die besonders in den figurenreichen Arbeiten gerne enthalten sind. Ein eindrucksvolles Beispiel hierfür liefert etwa die mit 2,50 auf 4,80 m bis dato größte Leinwand des Künstlers mit dem Titel »kausalkanon« (2018, Abb. S. 34 - 35). Hier versteckt sich im dichten Geflecht der typischen Schmittschen Bildelemente nicht nur ein Selbstbildniskopf oben links, es ist außerdem weiter unten noch zu lesen: »Kunst braucht Inhalte, Kunst braucht Betrachter die Kunst spüren« – ein Bekenntnis zum eigenen Schaffen. Wie eine Art »Kommentar« zum eigenen Künstlerdasein kann auch die Arbeit »nudelsiebtheoretiker« (2021, Abb. S. 131) gedeutet werden – der Künstler selbst fungiert als »Sieb«, das von Dingen der Außenwelt, des unmittelbaren Umraums durchströmt wird und sich vor diesen Einflüssen entweder verschließen oder sich ihnen öffnen kann, sie hindurch lässt, gleichsam gefiltert durch das eigene Innere. So heißt es auch im Bild »57« (2020, Abb. S. 85) in dem weiß auf schwarz handschriftlich geschriebenen Text »ich bin ein Nudelsieb«. Das Nudelsieb ist zweifellos Teil des persönlichen Symbolkanons, den aufmerksame Betrachter*innen in Schmitts Bildwelten wiederfinden können, auch das Farnblatt wäre hier zu nennen, ein scheinbar unauffälliges häufig wiederkehrendes Element – eine der wenigen Pflanzen, die einen sogenannten Generationenwechsel durchmacht bei dem ge-schlechtliche und ungeschlechtliche

exemplified by his frequent self-portraits, which are readily included, especially in the many-figure works. An impressive example of this is provided by the artist's largest canvas to date, at 2.50 by 4.80 meters, entitled »causal canon« (2018, fig. p. 34 - 35). Here, it is not only that a self-portrait of the artist's head is hidden at the top left among the dense mesh of his typical pictorial elements. In addition, further down the canvas one can read: »Art needs content, art needs viewers who feel the art« – an avowal of one's own creative work. The work »noodle colander theorist« (2021, fig. p. 131) can also be interpreted as a kind of »commentary« on one's own existence as an artist – the artist himself functions as a sieve through which things from the outside world, from the immediate surroundings, flow. He can either close himself off from these influences or open himself up to them, allowing them to pass through, filtered, as it were, through his own internal being. This is also what is said in picture »57« (2020, fig. p. 85) in the white-on-black handwritten text »I am a noodle sieve«. The noodle strainer is undoubtedly part of the personal canon of recurring symbols that the attentive viewer can find in Schmitt's pictorial worlds. The fern leaf should also be mentioned here, a seemingly inconspicuous, frequently recurring element. It is the only plant that undergoes a so-called alternation of generations and is for this very reason of particular importance to the artist, as something that harbors a secret not apparent at first glance.

Even if the artist himself is not included in the picture in the form of a self-portrait, his works always revolve around topics that concern him or have a close personal connection. Thus, aside from self-portraits, there are personal references, for example, to his Palatinate homeland – »potato noodle dove« (2019, fig. p. 65) – and to his own hobbies – »air lambrecht« (2021, fig. p. 123) – the artist plays basketball and has installed a basketball hoop in his spacious studio space. And then there are Schmitt's core topics alongside of art: biology, religion, philosophy. Relevant topics about which the artist sometimes likes to be

Fortpflanzung abwechseln und die Mutterpflanze komplett anders aussieht als ihre Nachkommen. Gerade deshalb ist sie für den Künstler von besonderer Bedeutung, als ein Symbol für etwas, das sich wandelt und verändert und ein Geheimnis birgt, welches auf den ersten Blick nicht ersichtlich ist.

Auch wenn der Künstler selbst nicht in Form eines Selbstporträts im Bild enthalten ist, so kreisen seine Arbeiten doch stets um Themen, die ihn betreffen oder einen engen persönlichen Bezug aufweisen. So gibt es neben dem Selbstbildnis persönliche Referenzen, etwa an die Pfälzer Heimat – »schupfnudeltaube« (2019, Abb. S. 65) – und eigene Hobbies – »air lambrecht« (2021, Abb. S. 123) – der Künstler ist Basketballer und hat entsprechend auch einen Basketballkorb in seiner großzügigen Atelierhalle angebracht. Und dann Schmitts Kern-Themen neben der Kunst: Biologie, Religion, Philosophie. Relevante Themen, mit denen der Künstler gerne auch mal provoziert, besonders über Fragen des Glaubens und der Religion, etwa in großformatigen Bildern wie »du sollst nicht denken« (2019, Abb. S. 50 - 51) mit einem gekreuzigten Mensch-Tier-Wesen im Mittelpunkt, das eindeutig weiblichen Geschlechts ist oder »adam und edamer« (2020, Abb. S. 107), in dem biblische Inhalte mit Darwin und der Evolutionsgeschichte konfrontiert werden. Kunst braucht Inhalte – Inhalte, die Fragen stellen, ohne aber Antworten vorzugeben oder eingefahrenen Wegen zu folgen. Hier macht einer nicht das, was andere sehen wollen oder was der Markt bestimmt, sondern bleibt bei sich, macht sein eigenes Ding, ohne sich beirren zu lassen und gerade das hat Erfolg.

provocative, especially on questions of faith and religion. For example, in large-format paintings such as »you shalt not think« (2019, fig. p. 50 - 51) with a crucified human–animal being at its center that is clearly female, or »adam and edam« (2020, fig. p. 107), in which biblical content is confronted with Darwin and the history of evolution. Art needs content – content that asks questions, but without prescribing answers or following well-worn paths. Here, we have someone who does not do what others want to see or what the market dictates, but stays within himself, doing his own thing, undeterred – and that is precisely what brings success.

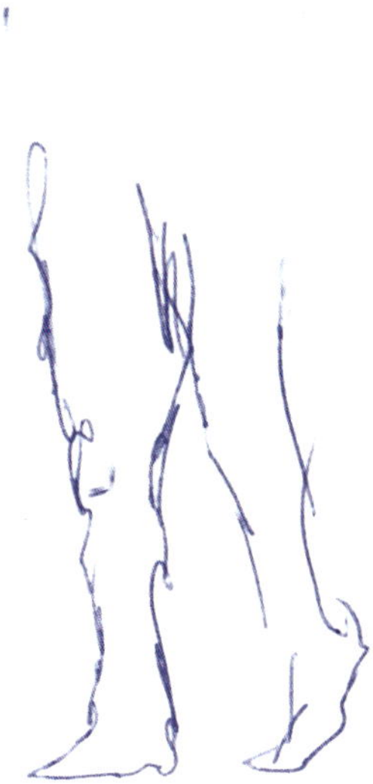

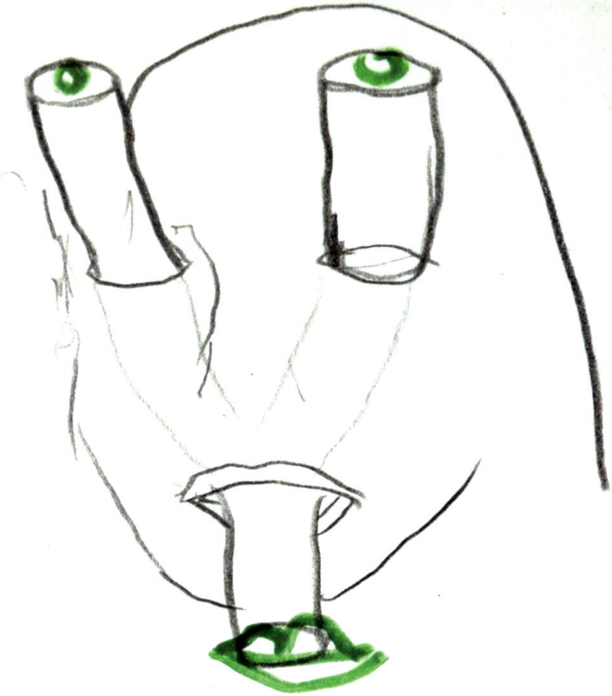

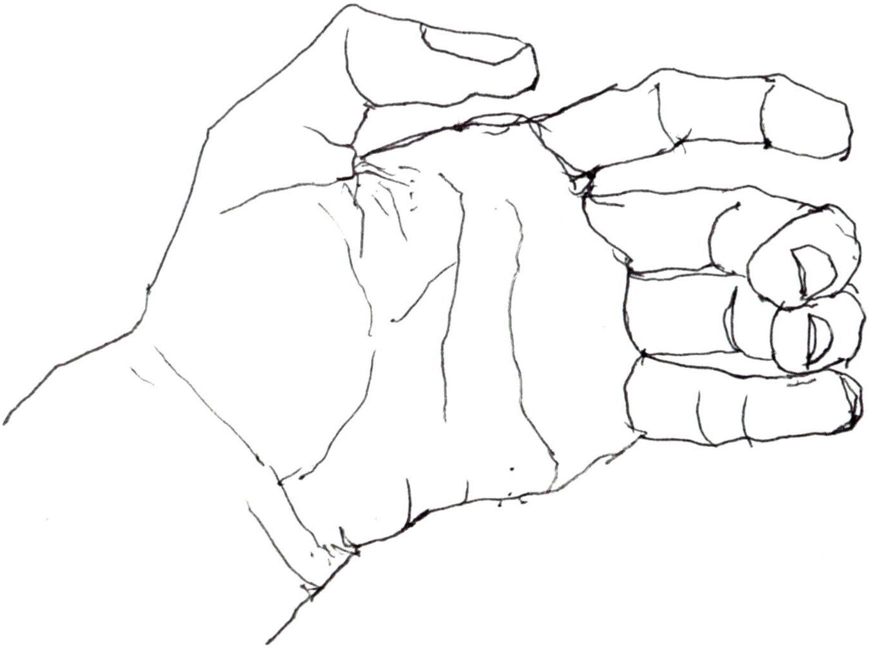

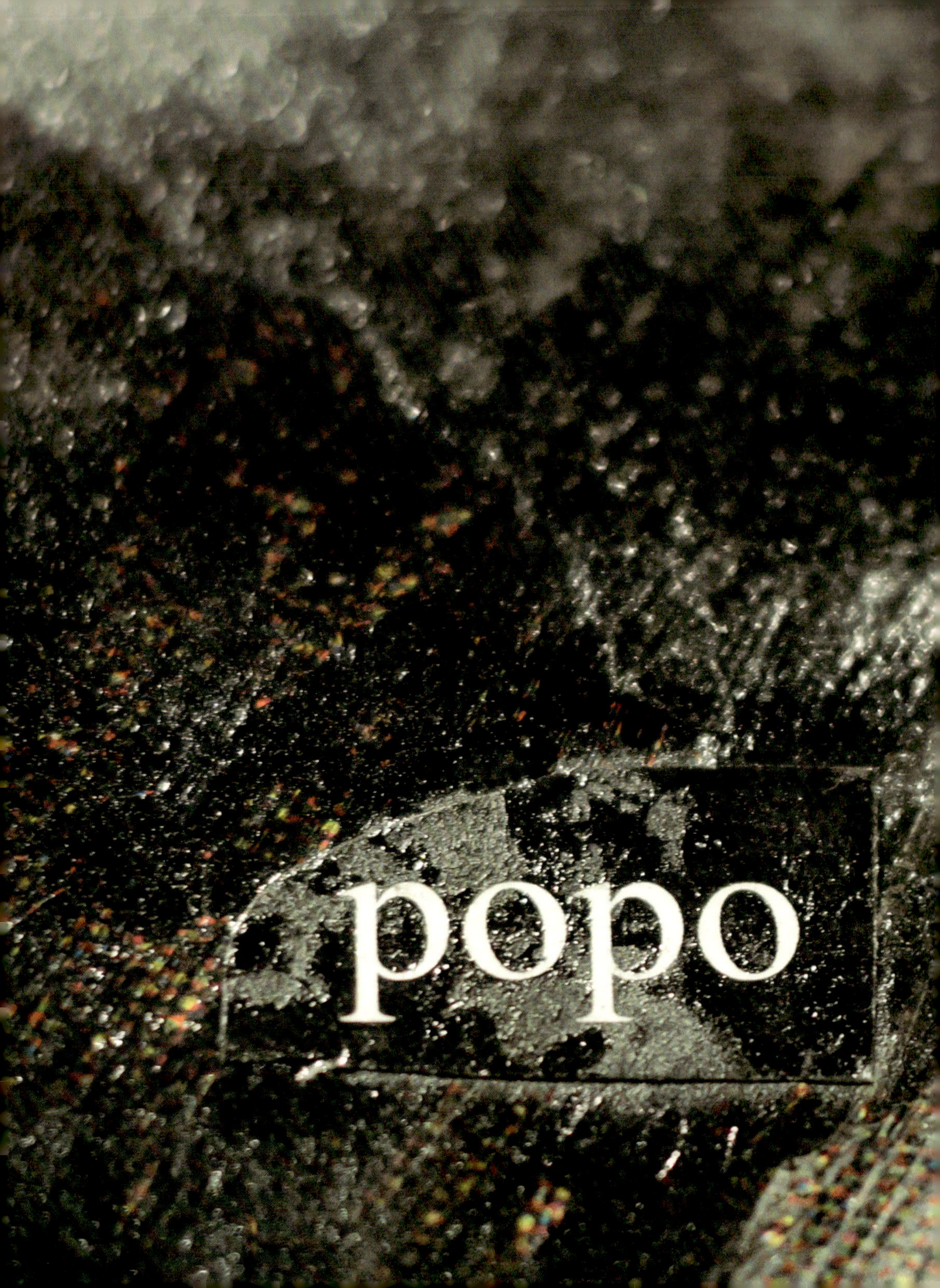
popo

leer | empty

2017, Mixed Media on Canvas, 60 x 50 cm
Privatsammlung Österreich | Private Collection Austria

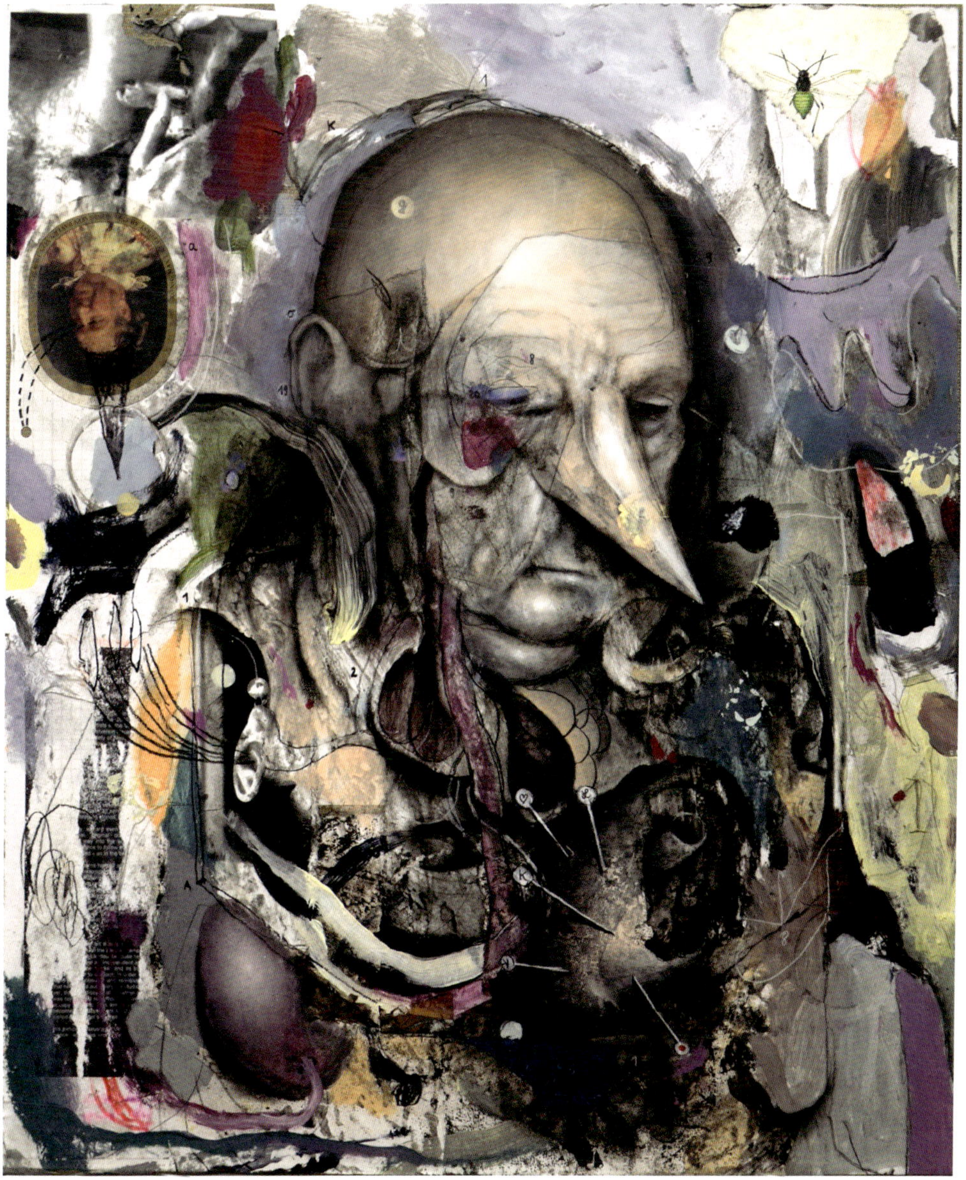

fielvlügelphalter | many-winged moth

2017, Mixed Media on Canvas, 60 x 50 cm
Privatsammlung Deutschland | Private Collection Germany

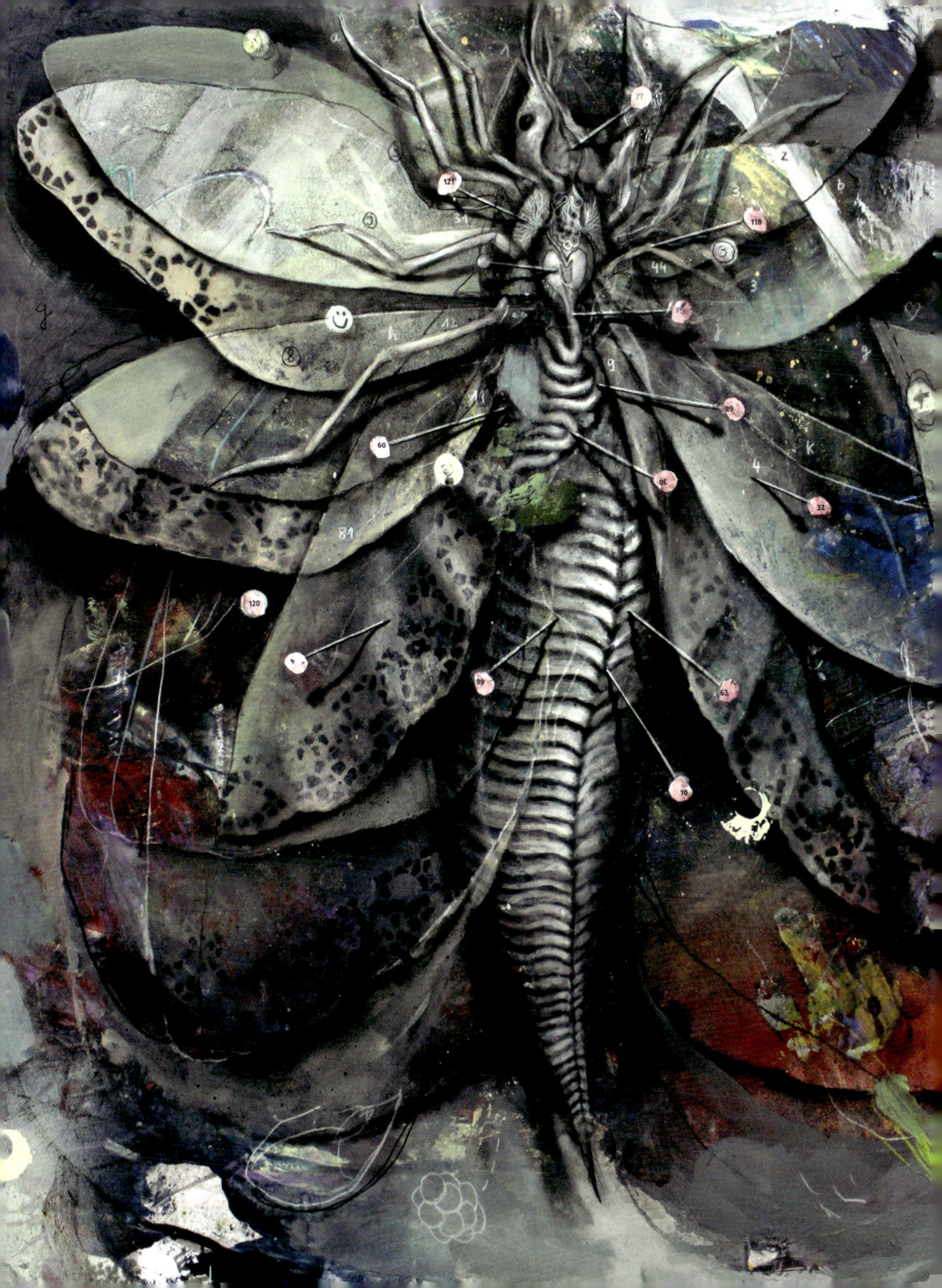

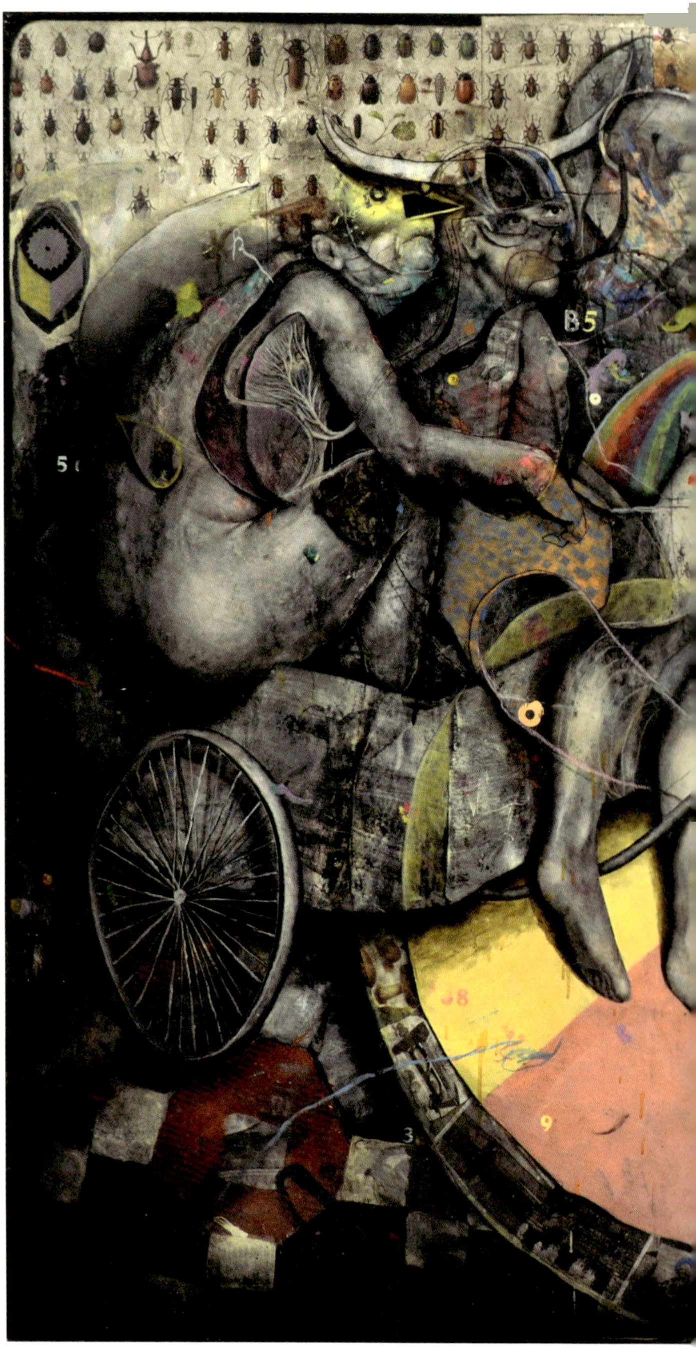

karawane (share what you wiederkäu)
caravan (share what you ruminate)

2017, Mixed Media on Canvas, 180 x 250 cm
Privatsammlung Spanien
Private Collection Spain

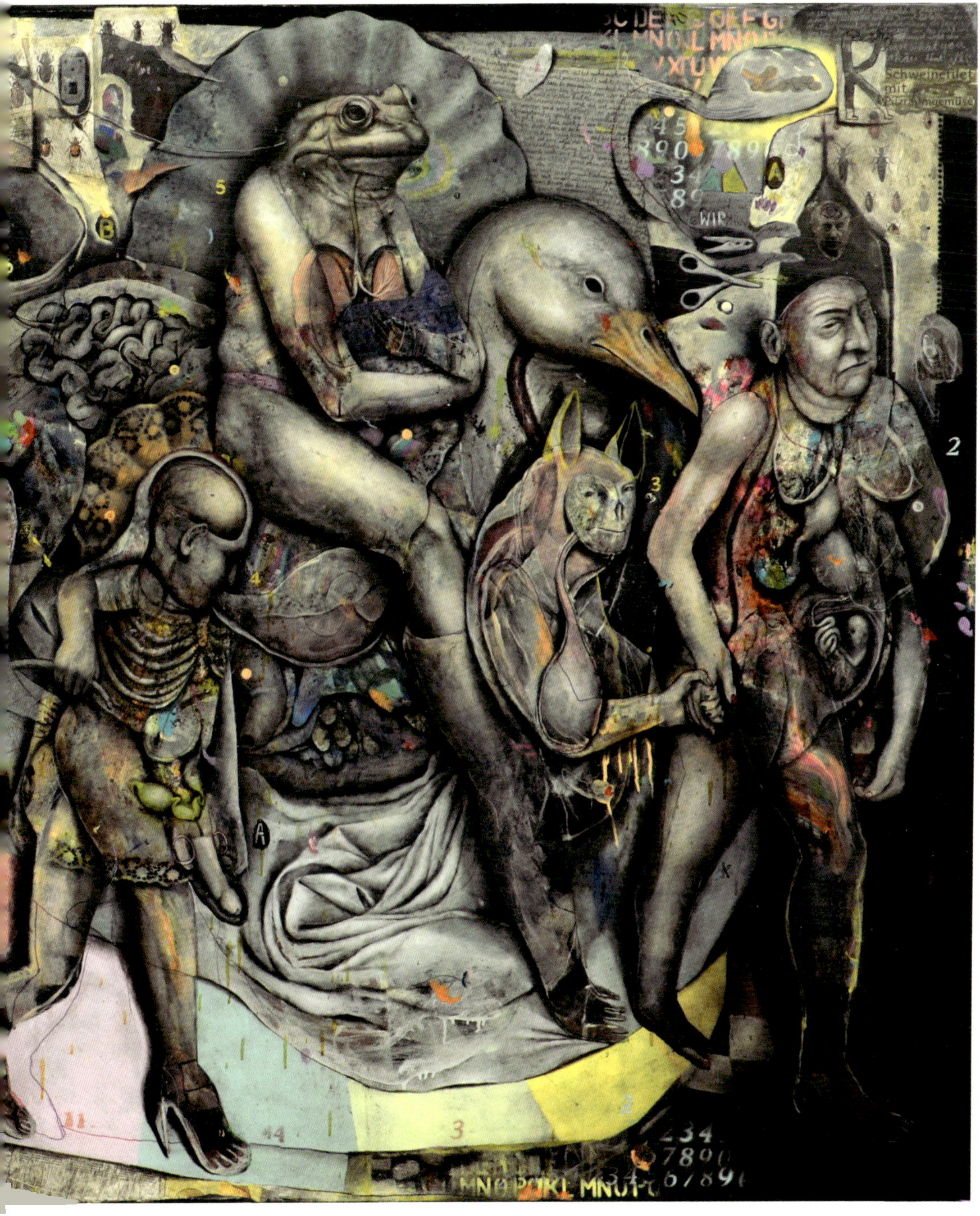
Schweinefilet
mit
WIR

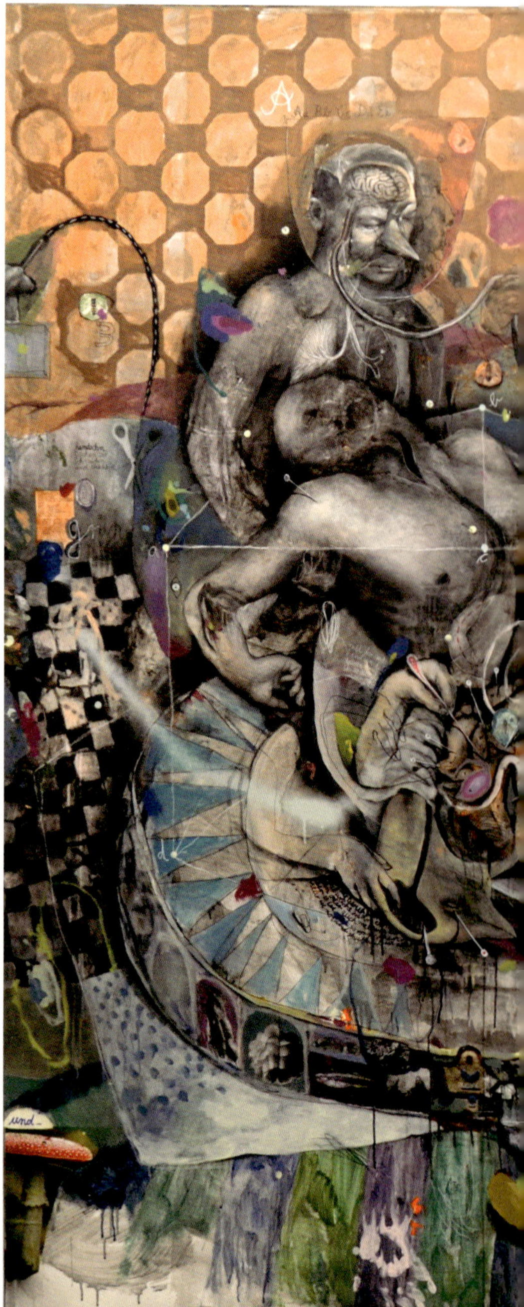

zufall und notwendigkeit | coincidence and necessity

2017, Mixed Media on Canvas, 250 x 360 cm
Privatsammlung Spanien | Private Collection Spain

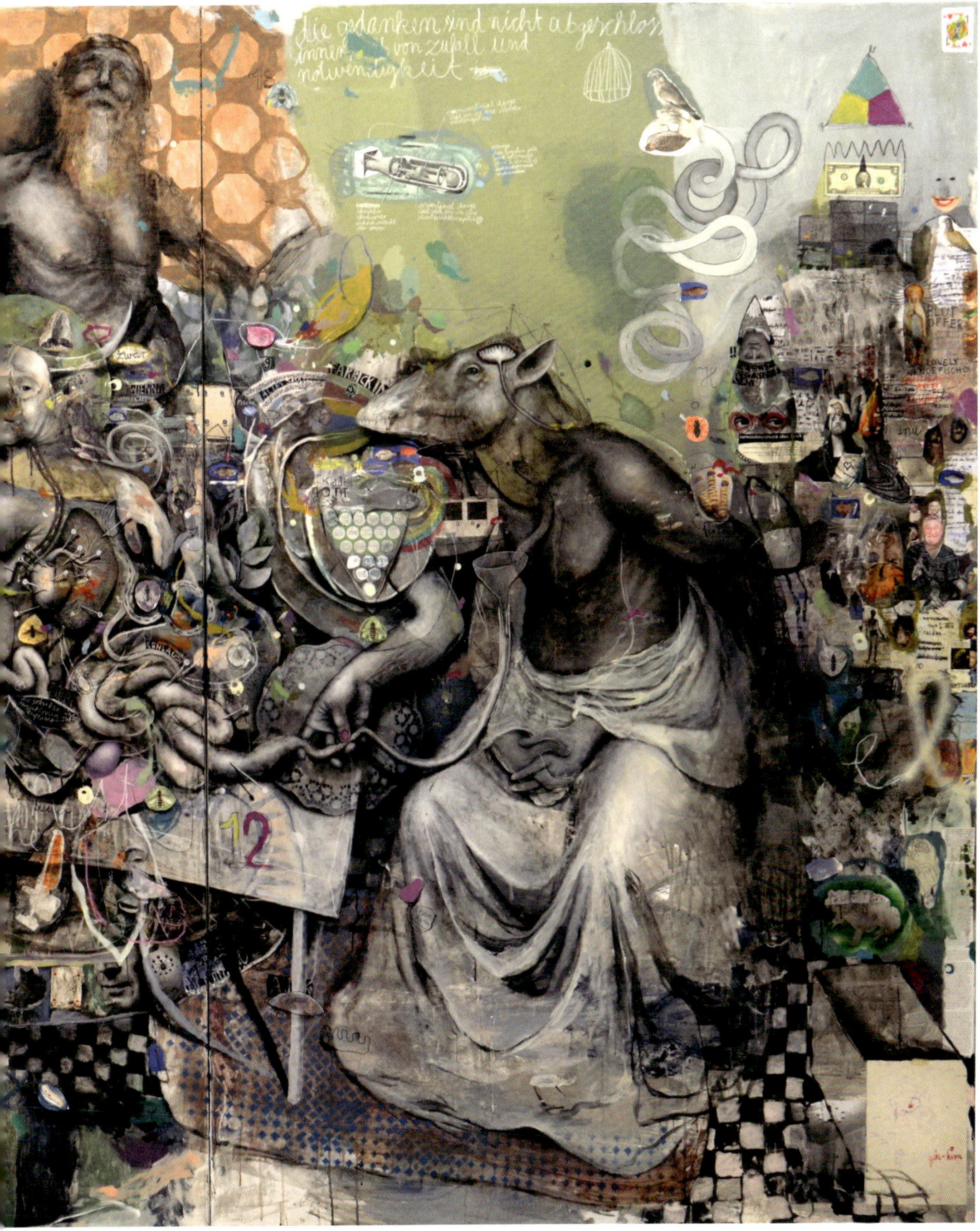
die gedanken sind nicht abgeschloss
von zufall und
notwendigkeit

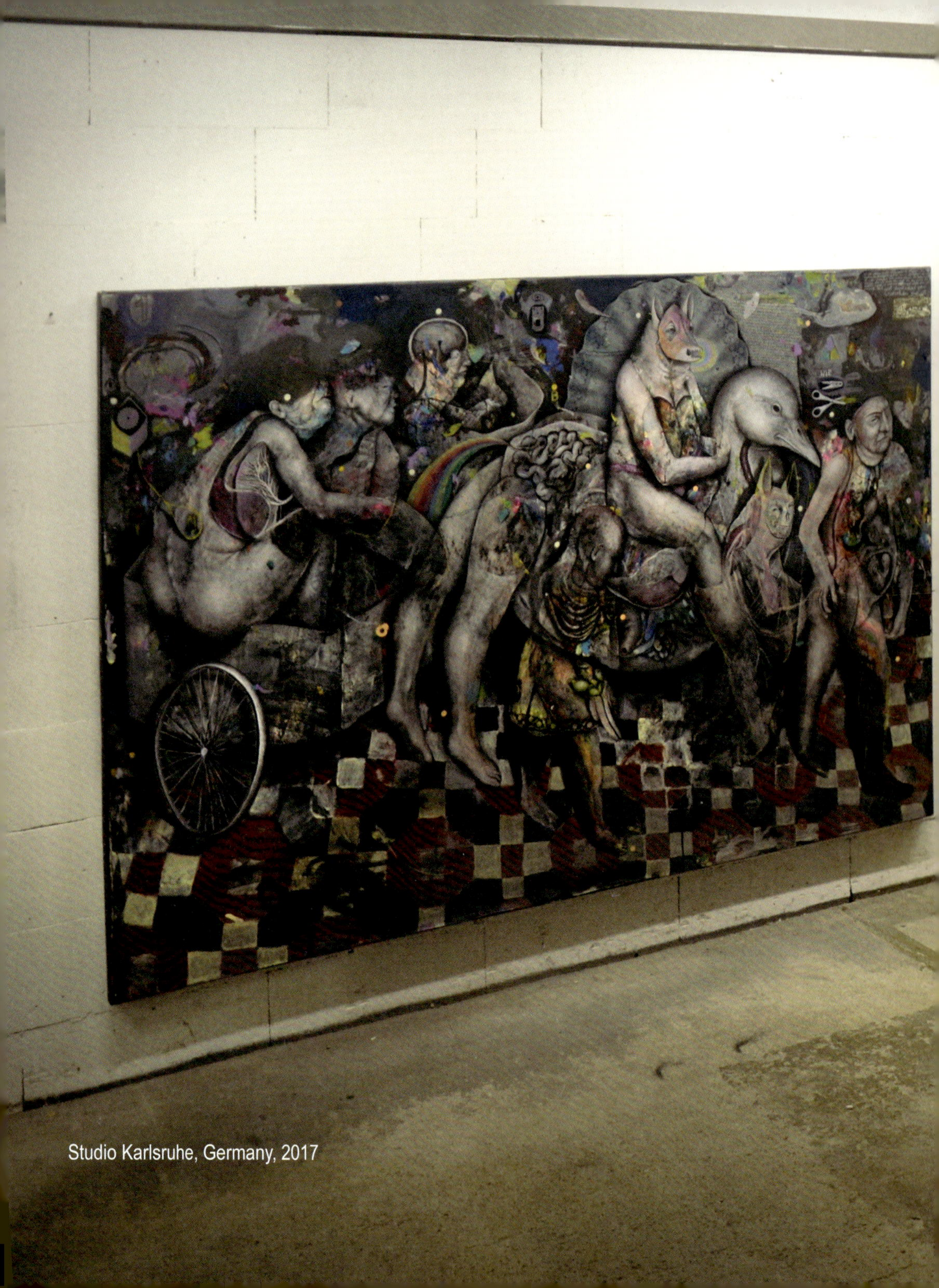

Studio Karlsruhe, Germany, 2017

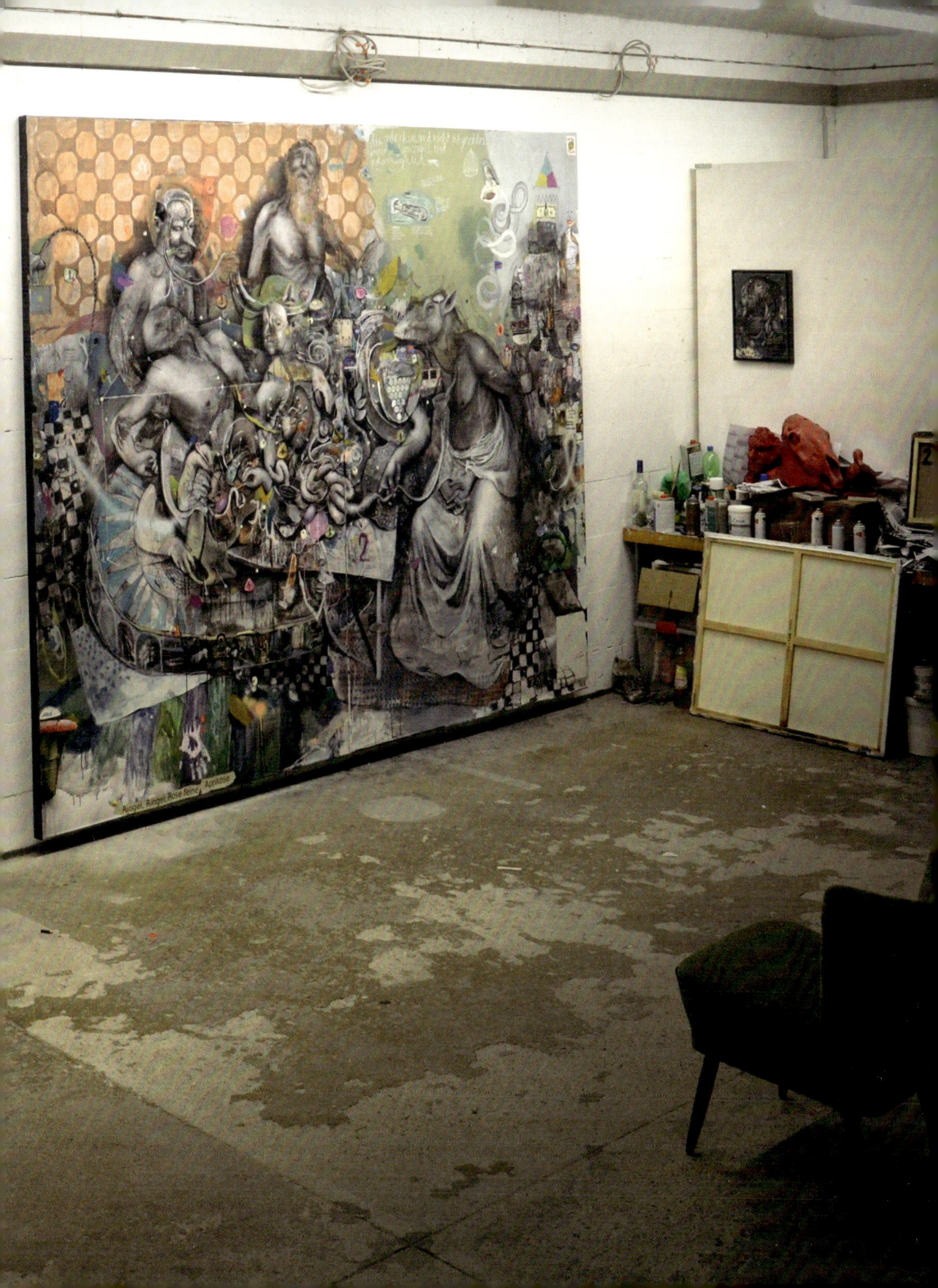
Ringel, Ringel, Rose feine, Aprikose

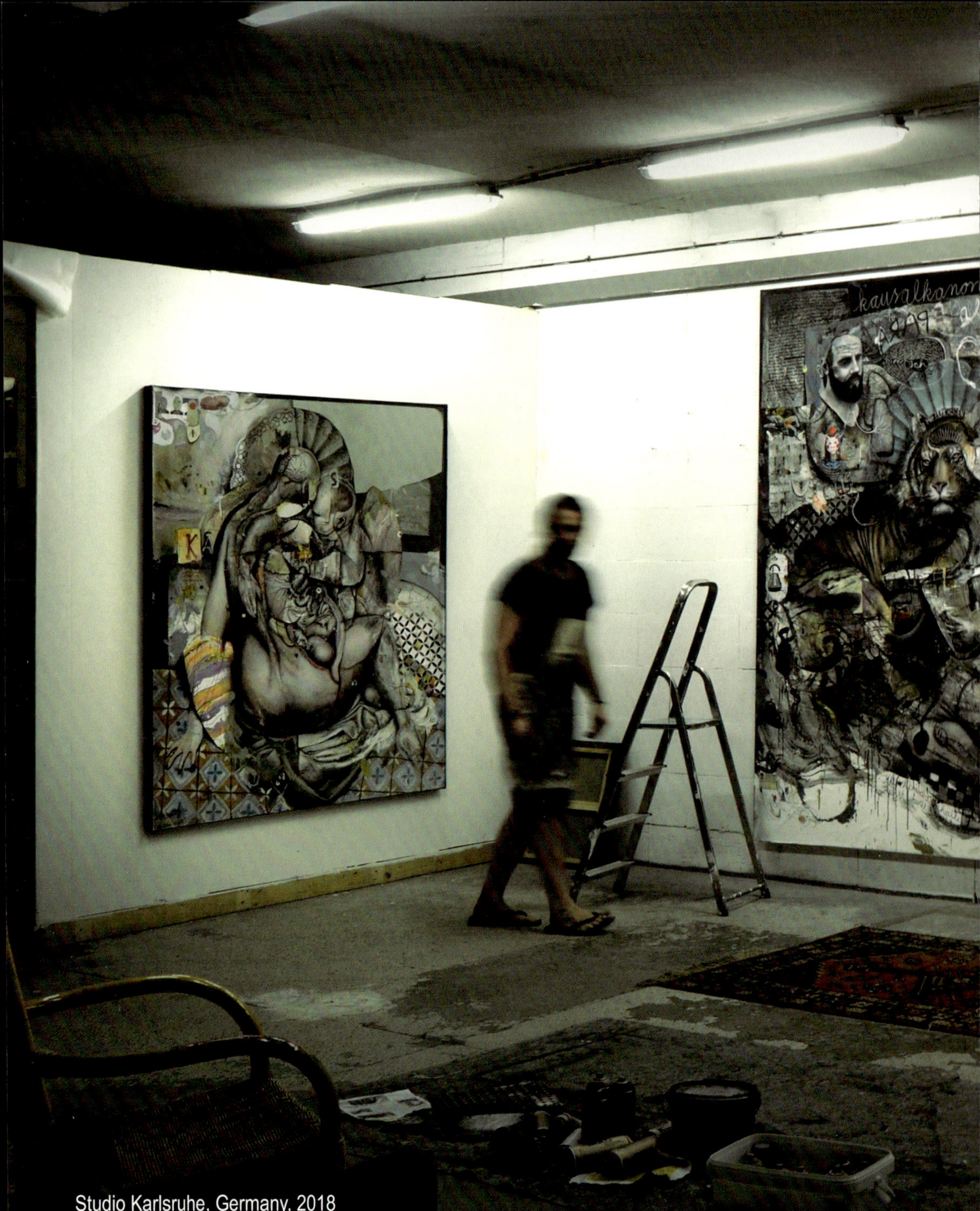

Studio Karlsruhe, Germany, 2018

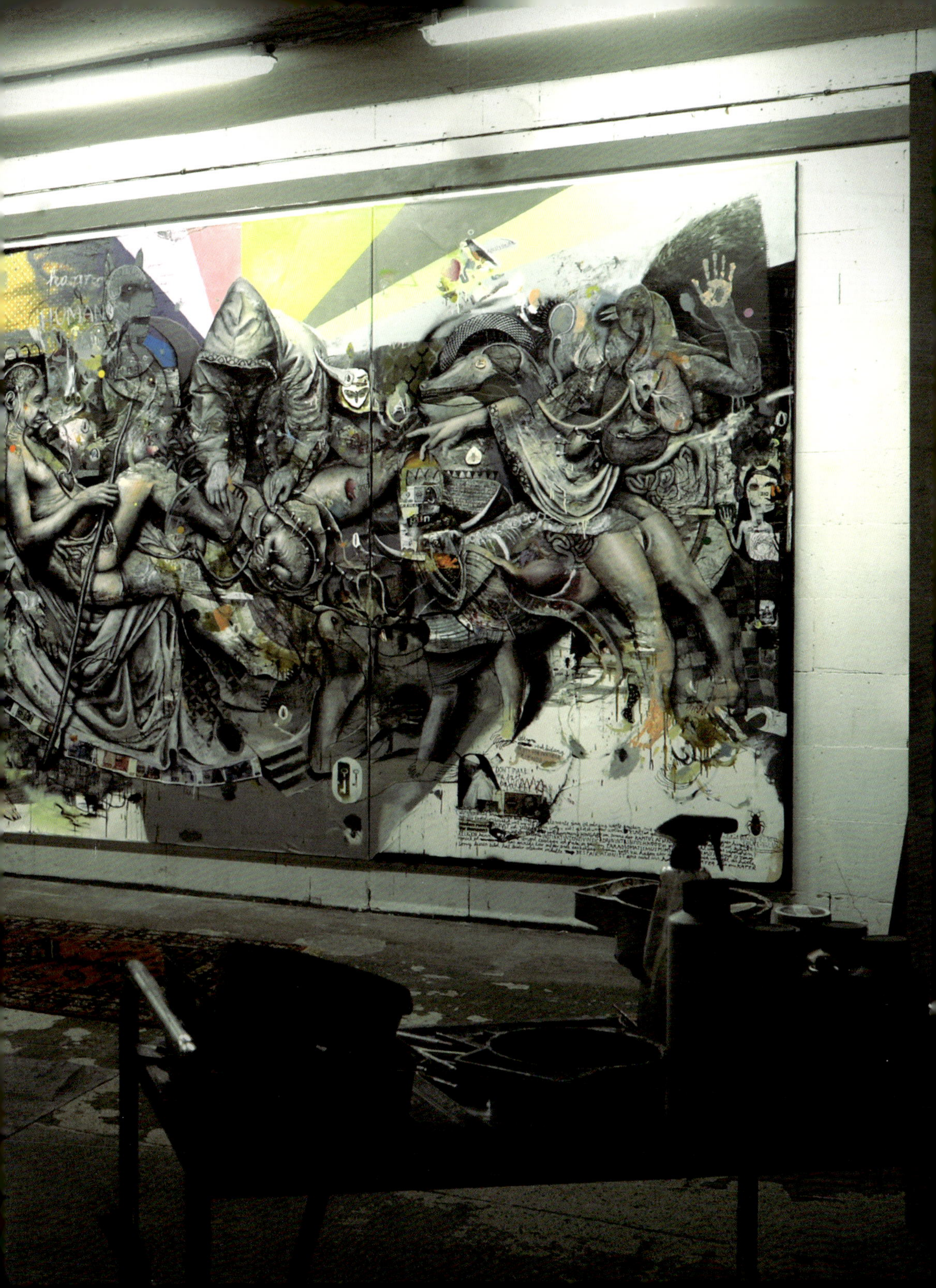

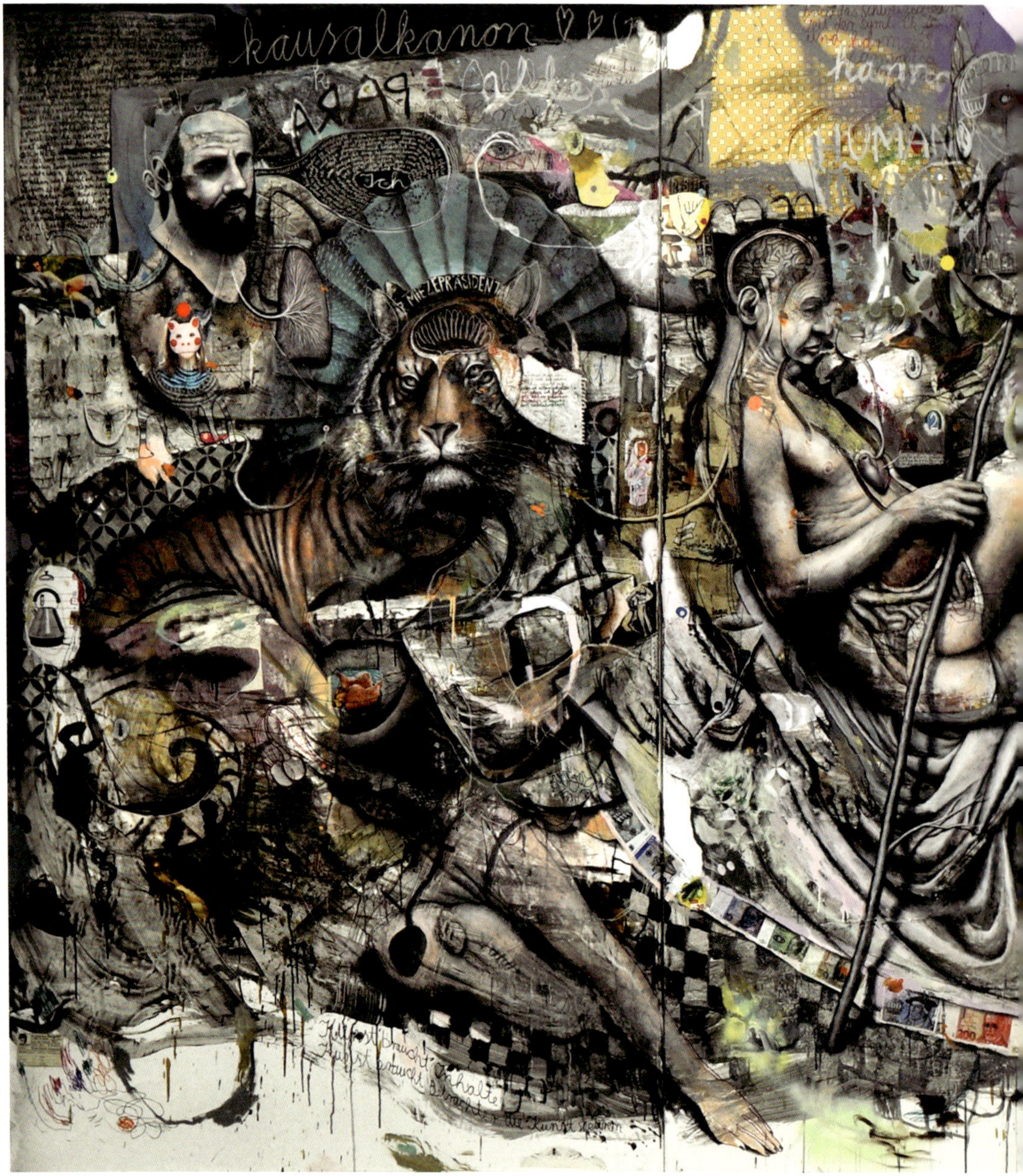

kausalkanon | causal canon

2018, Mixed Media on Canvas, 250 x 480 cm
Privatsammlung Österreich | Private Collection Austria

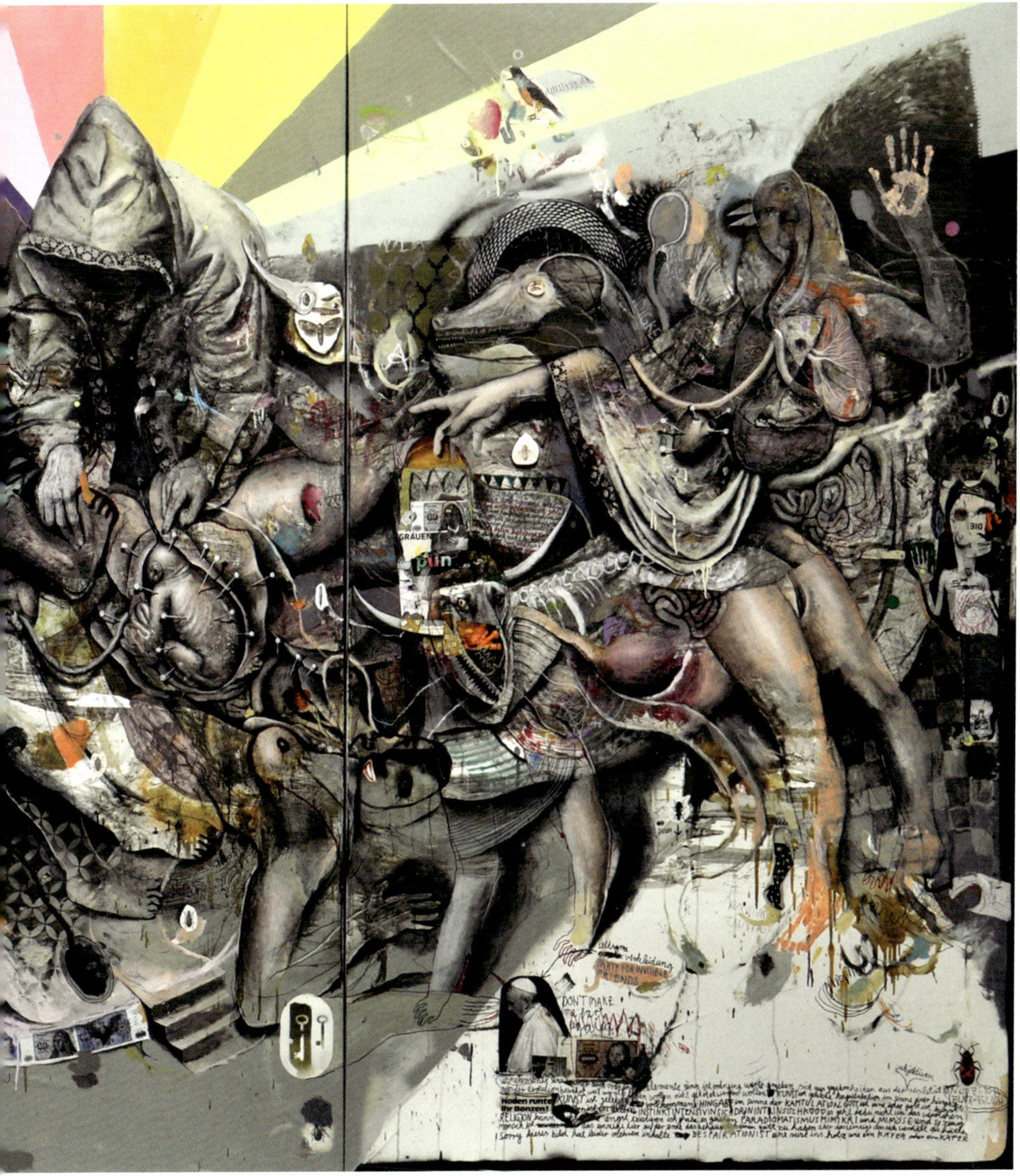
GRAUEN
DON'T MAKE
Hoden runter
ihr Bonzen!
DESPAIRATIONIST

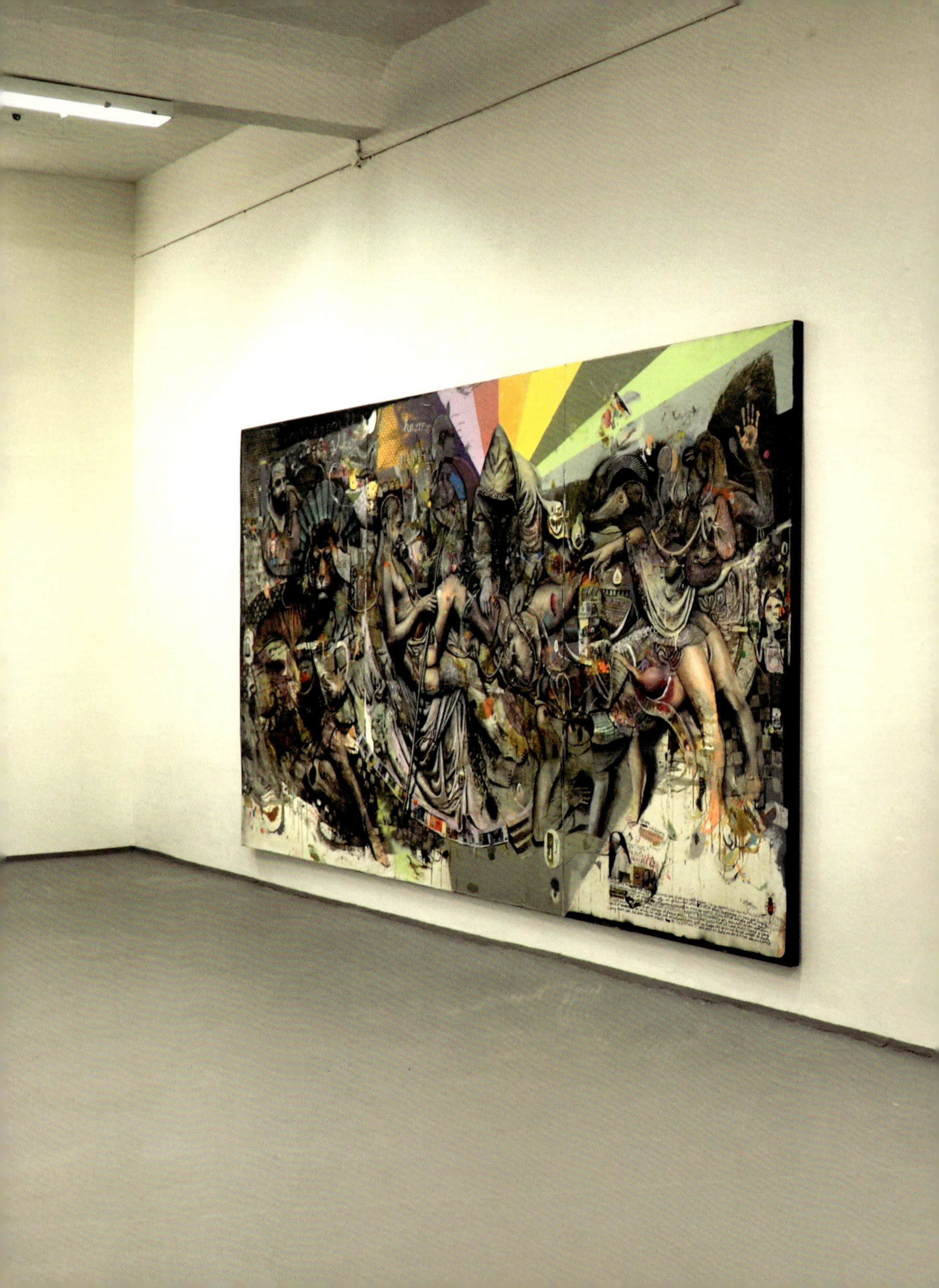

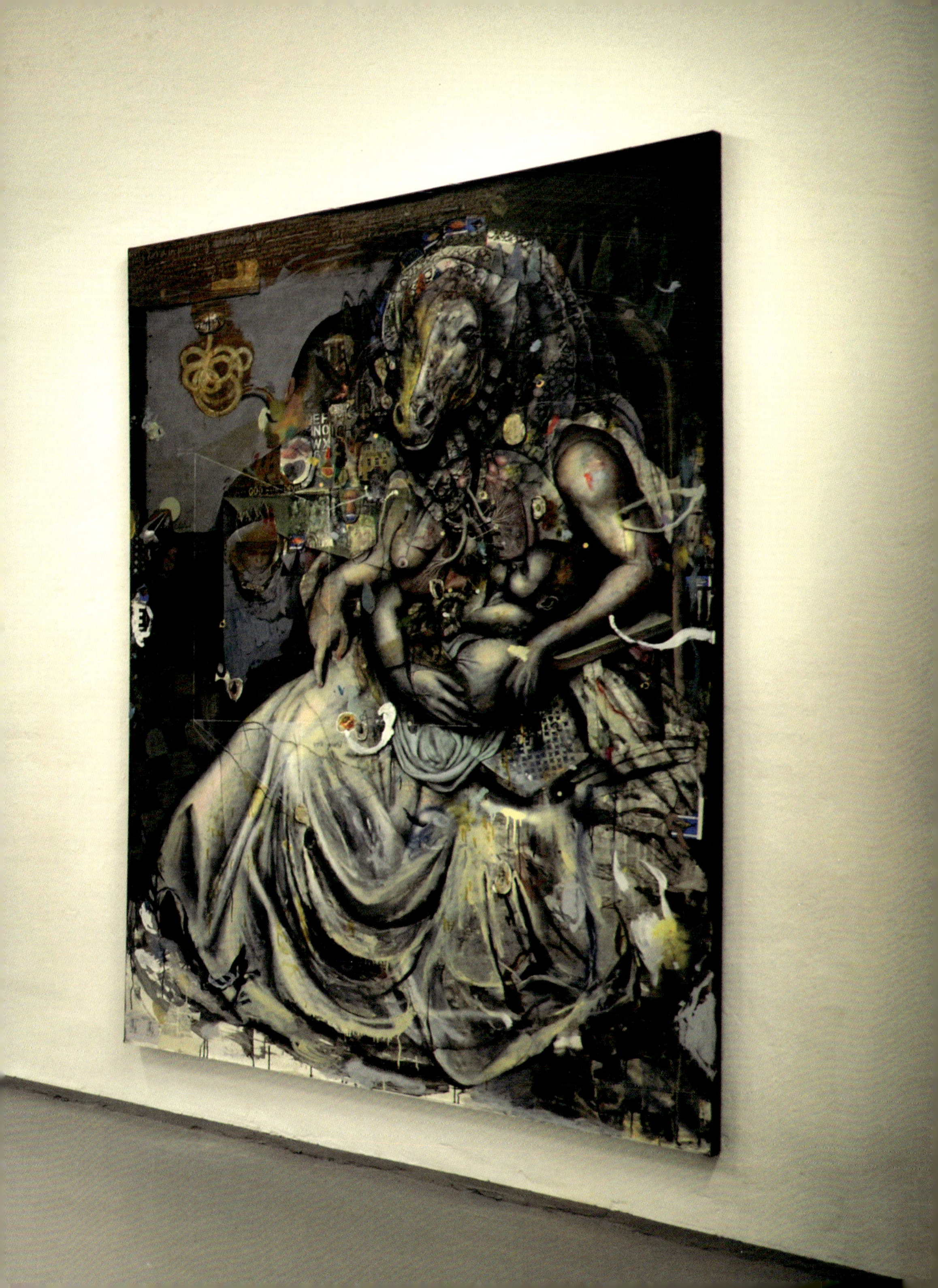

büchsenwühler | tin-can rummager

2018, Mixed Media on Canvas, 60 x 50 cm
Privatsammlung Schweiz | Private Collection Switzerland

Vorherige Seite / Previous Page

Soloshow, »kausalkanon«,
Galerie Thomas Hühsam, Offenbach am Main, Germany, 2018

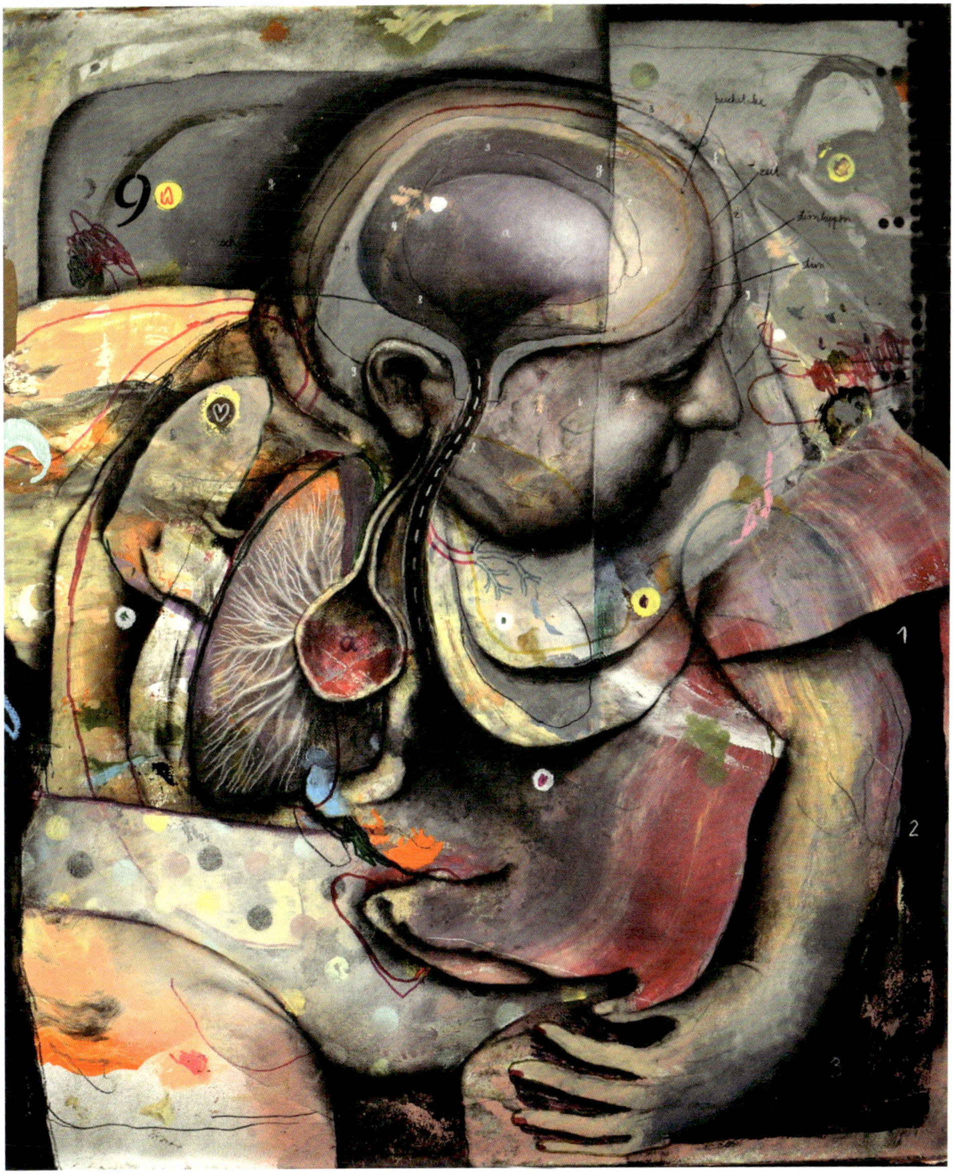

hirschgänger (im zweifel) | deer walker (in doubt)

2018, Mixed Media on Canvas, 60 x 50 cm
Privatsammlung Deutschland | Private Collection Germany

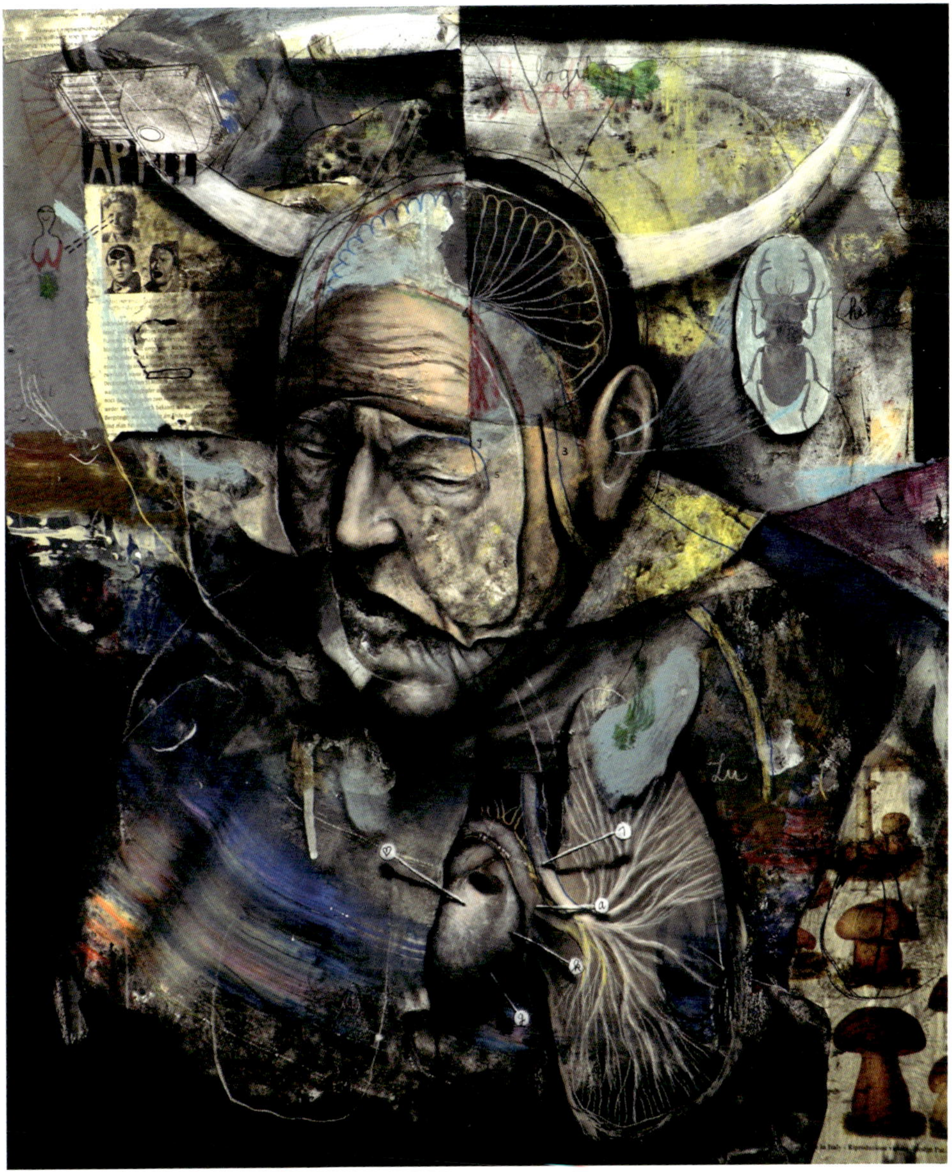

abendlichtsammler | evening light collector

2018, Mixed Media on Canvas, 60 x 50 cm
Privatsammlung Deutschland | Private Collection Germany

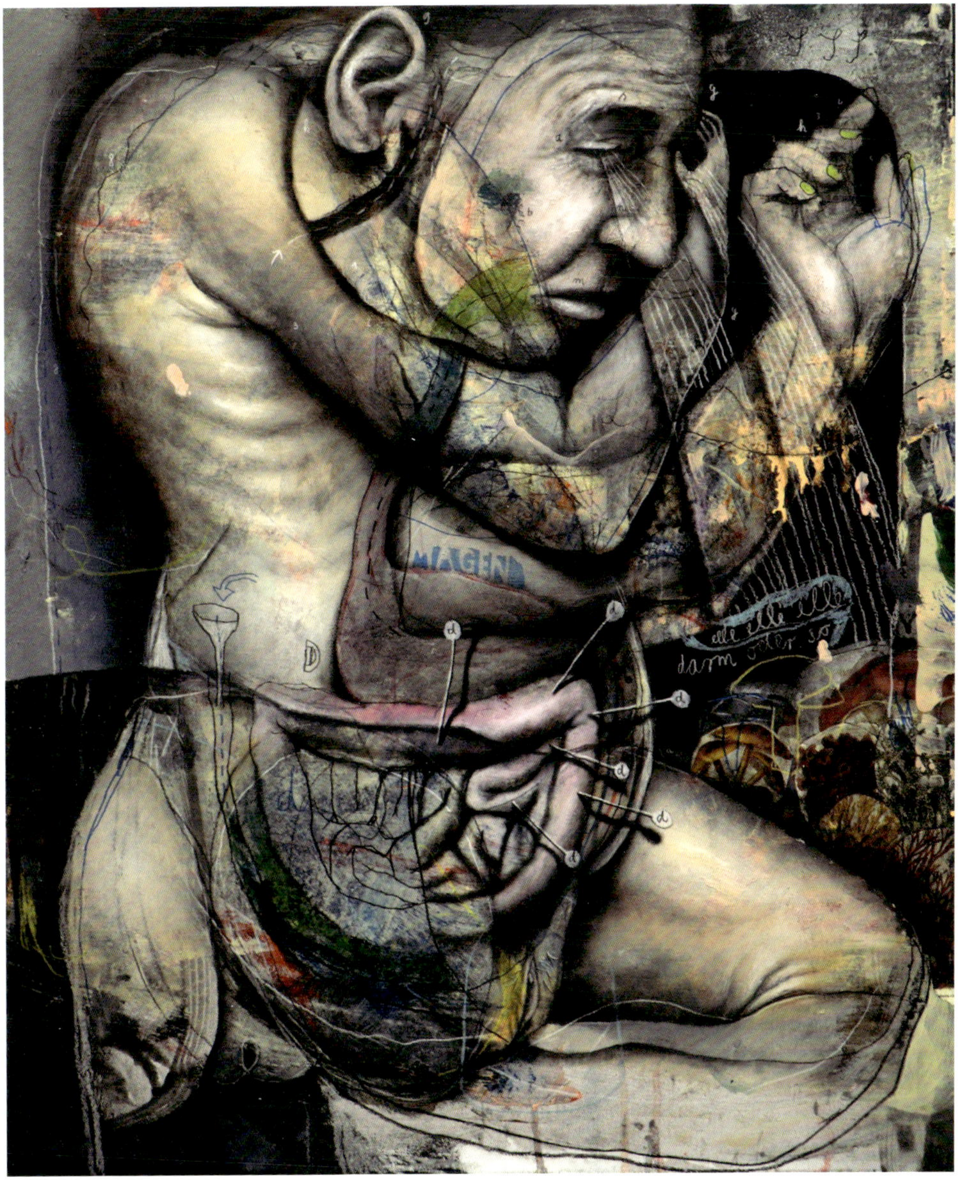
MAGEN
elle elle elle
darm oder so

dark duck-doc-dog

2018, Mixed Media on Canvas, 60 x 50 cm

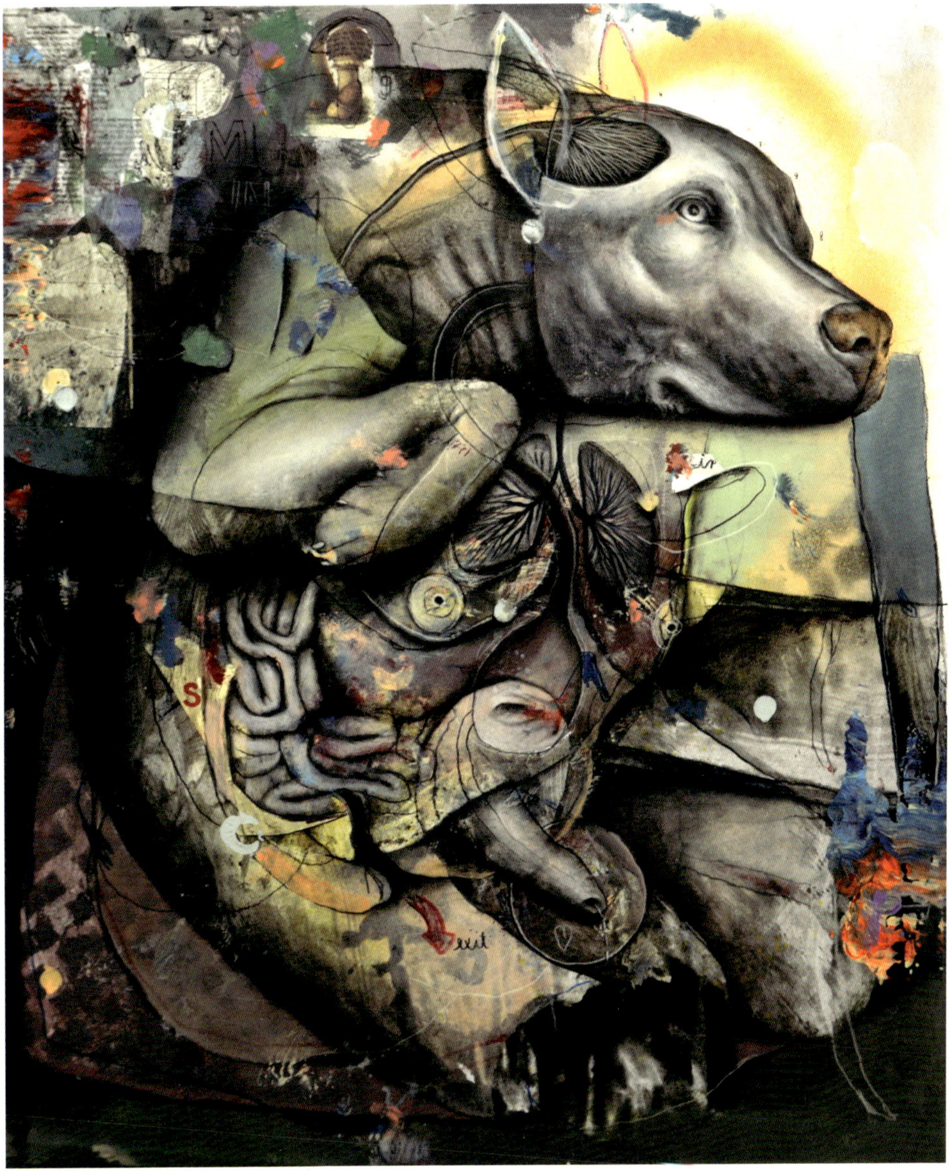

stöckelgans | stiletto goose

2018, Mixed Media on Canvas, 60 x 50 cm
Privatsammlung Schweiz | Private Collection Switzerland

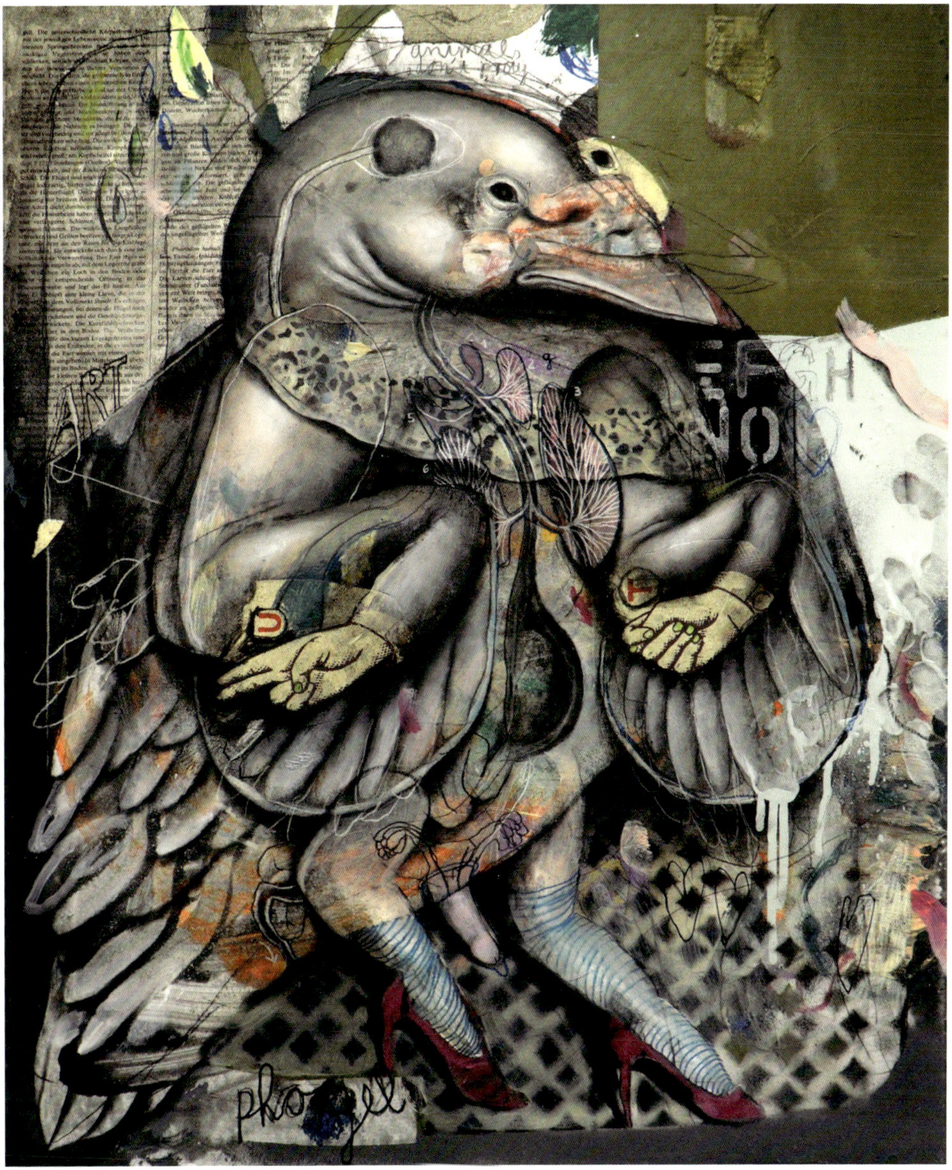

pferd | horse

2018, Mixed Media on Canvas, 250 x 170 cm
Privatsammlung Deutschland | Private Collection Germany

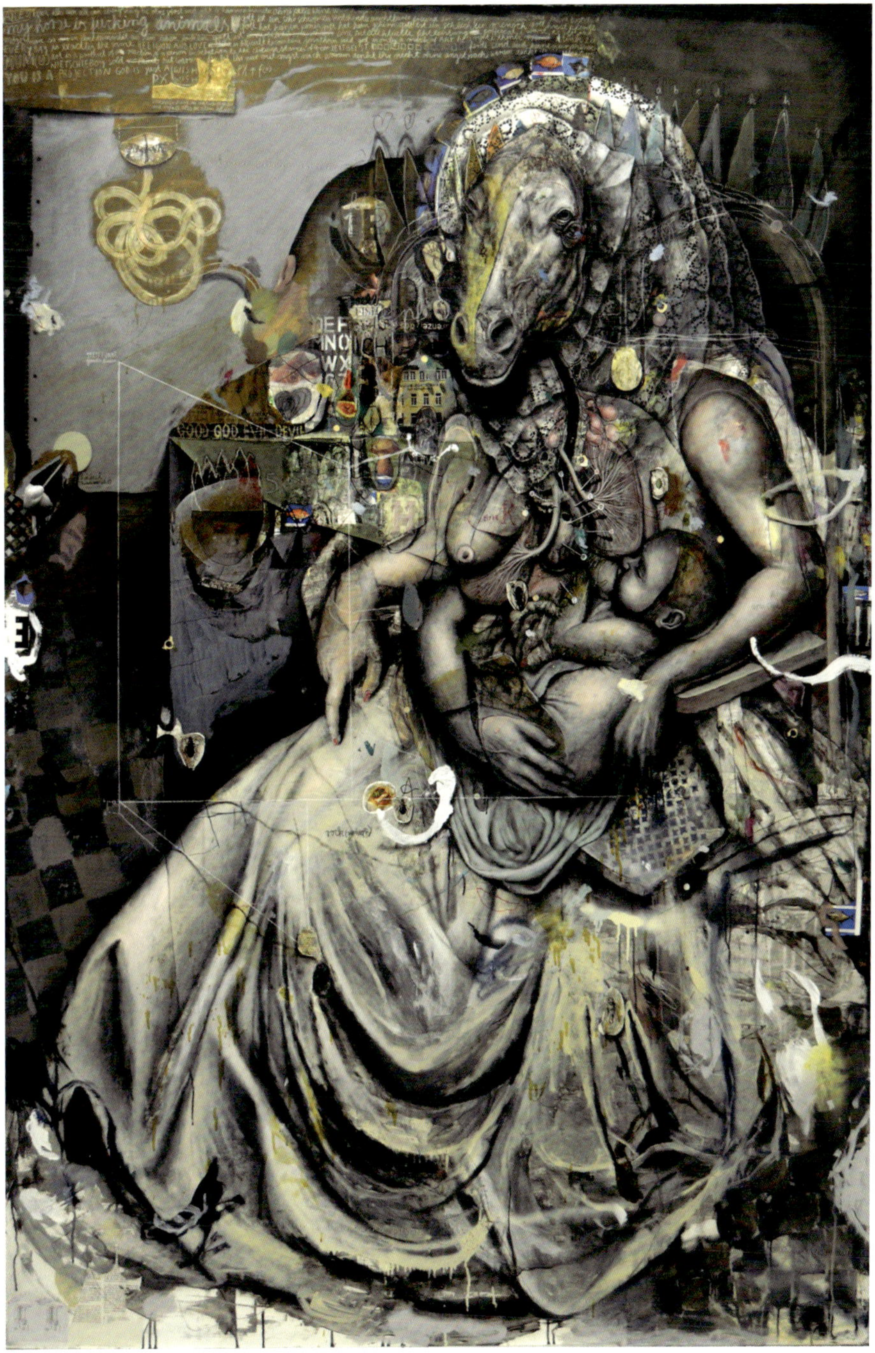

GOOD GOD EVIL DEVIL

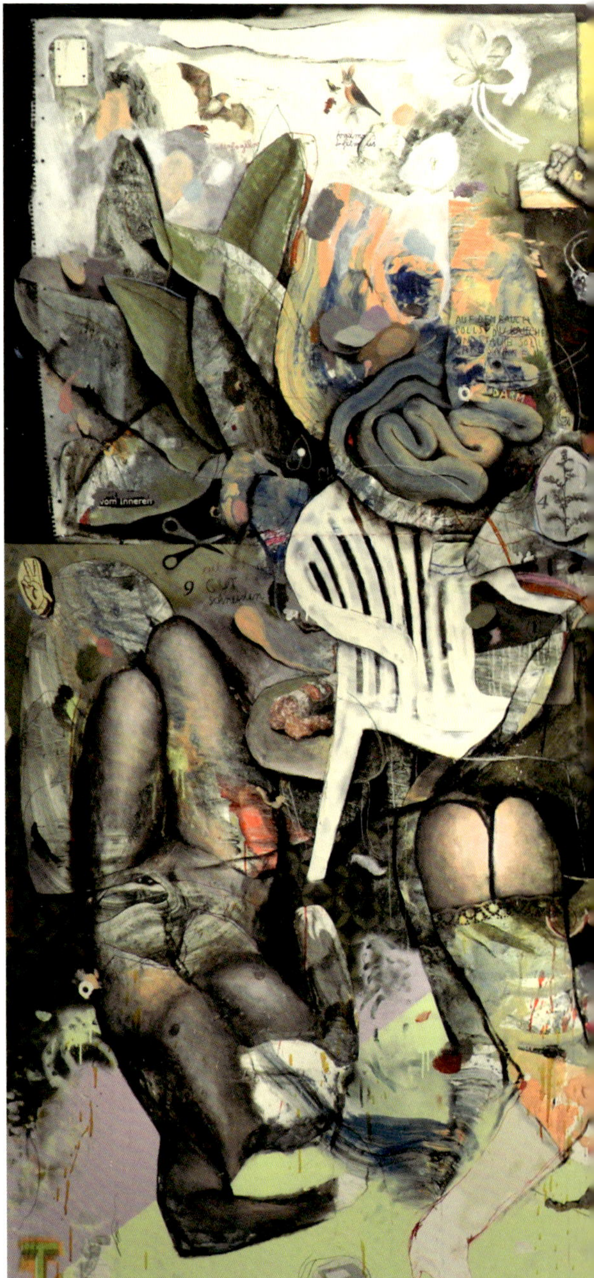

du sollst nicht denken | you shalt not think

2018, Mixed Media on Canvas, 250 x 340 cm
Privatsammlung Deutschland | Private Collection Germany

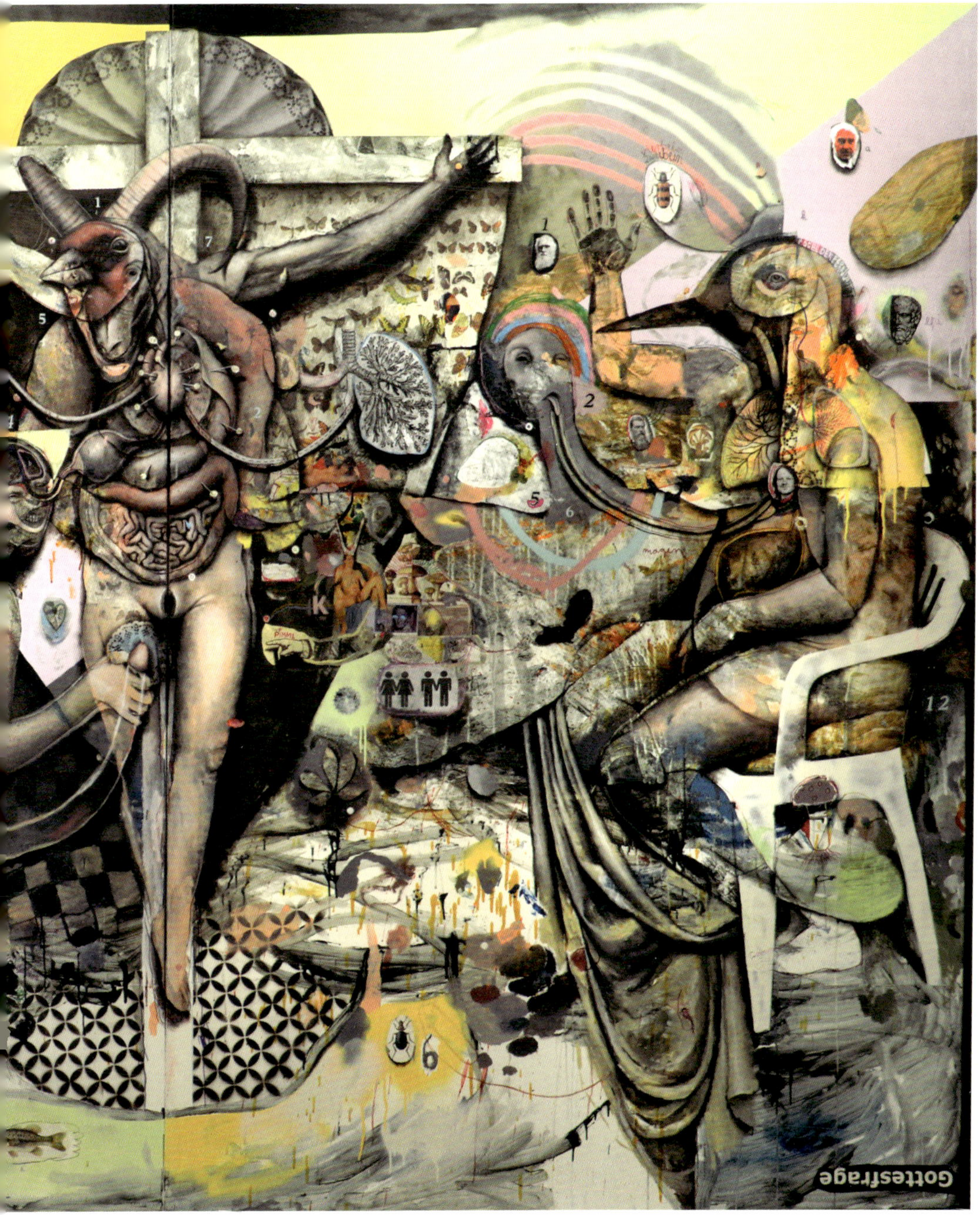

der fette löwe | the fat lion

2018, Mixed Media on Canvas, 250 x 180 cm
Privatsammlung Österreich | Private Collection Austria

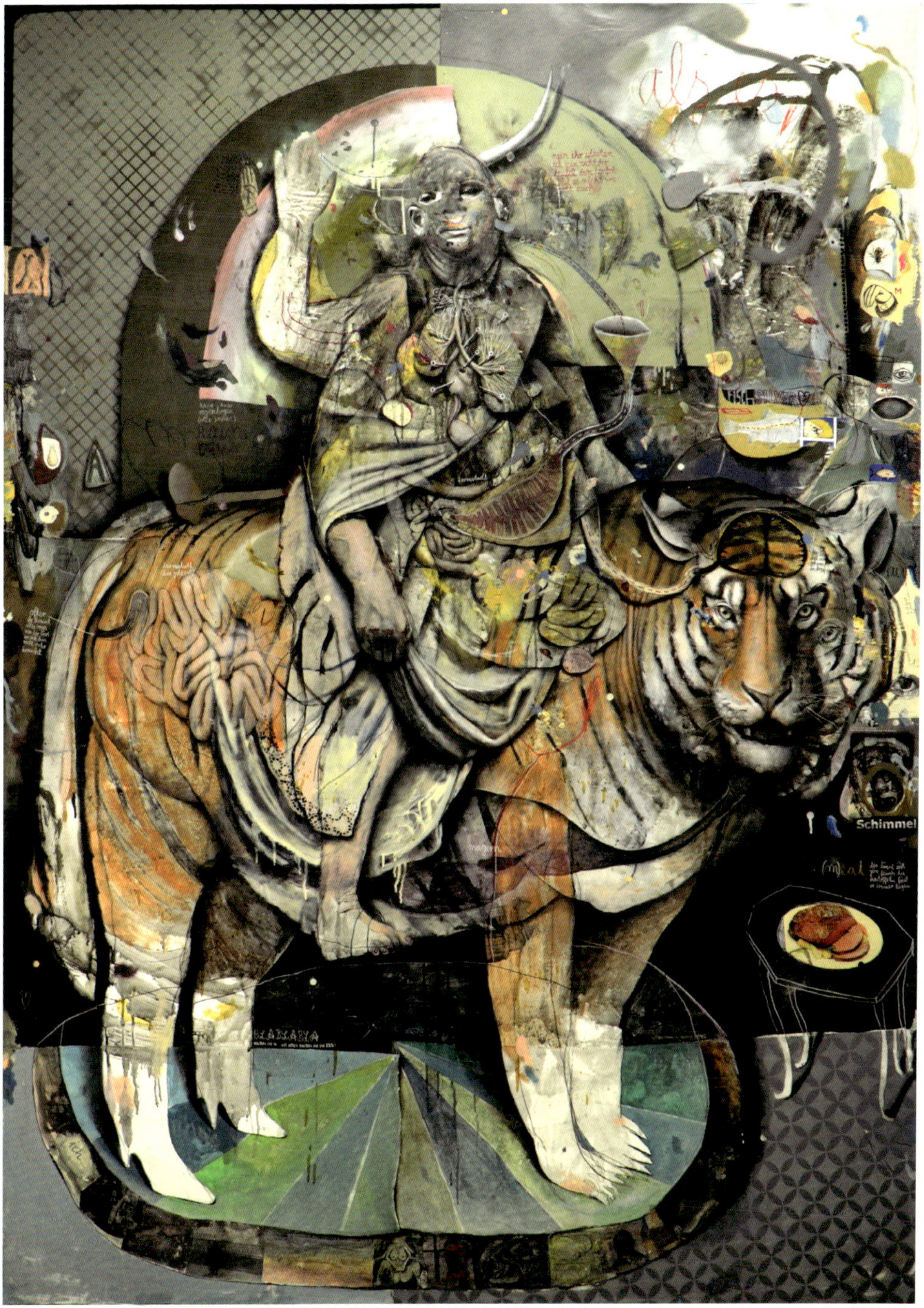
Schimmel

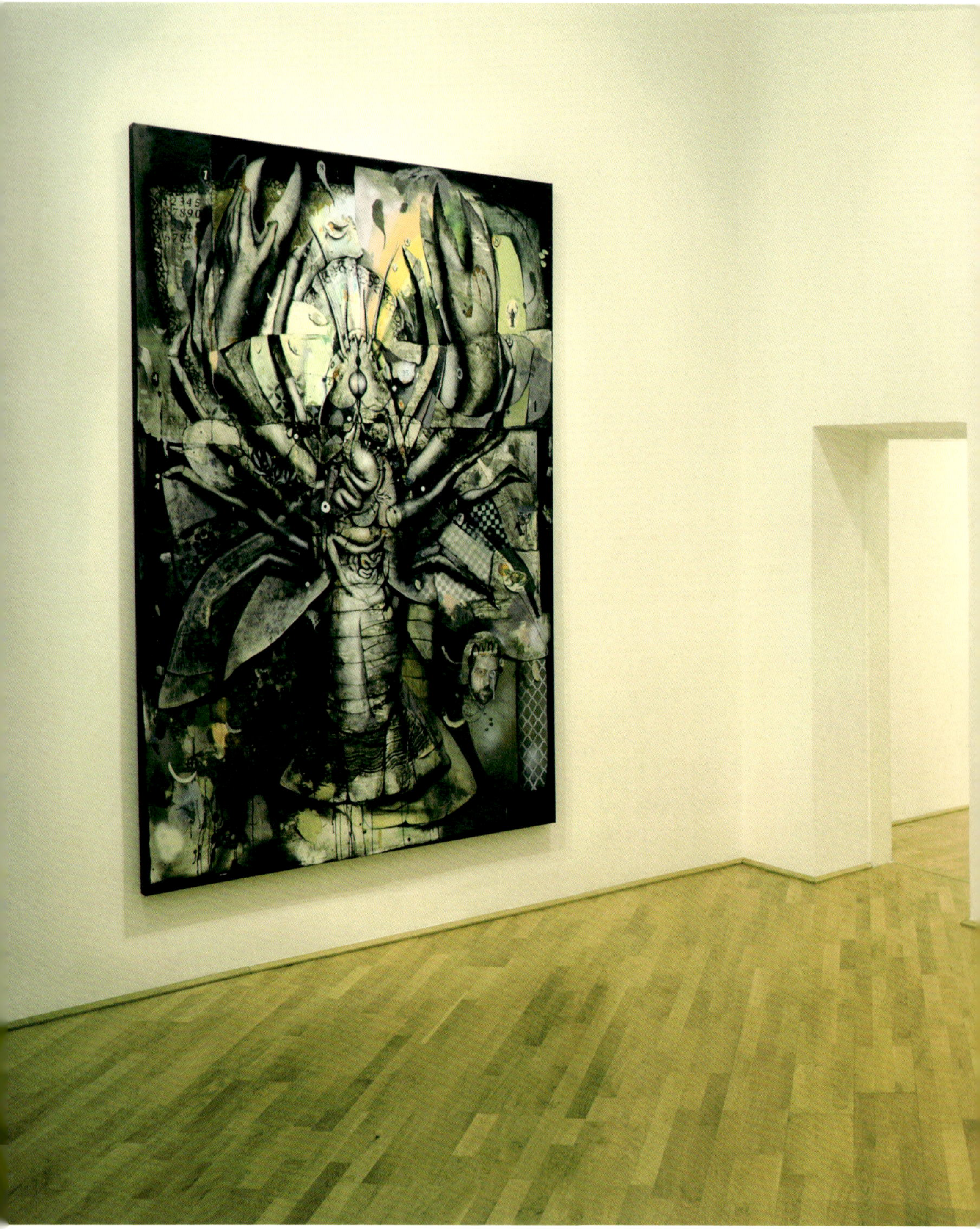

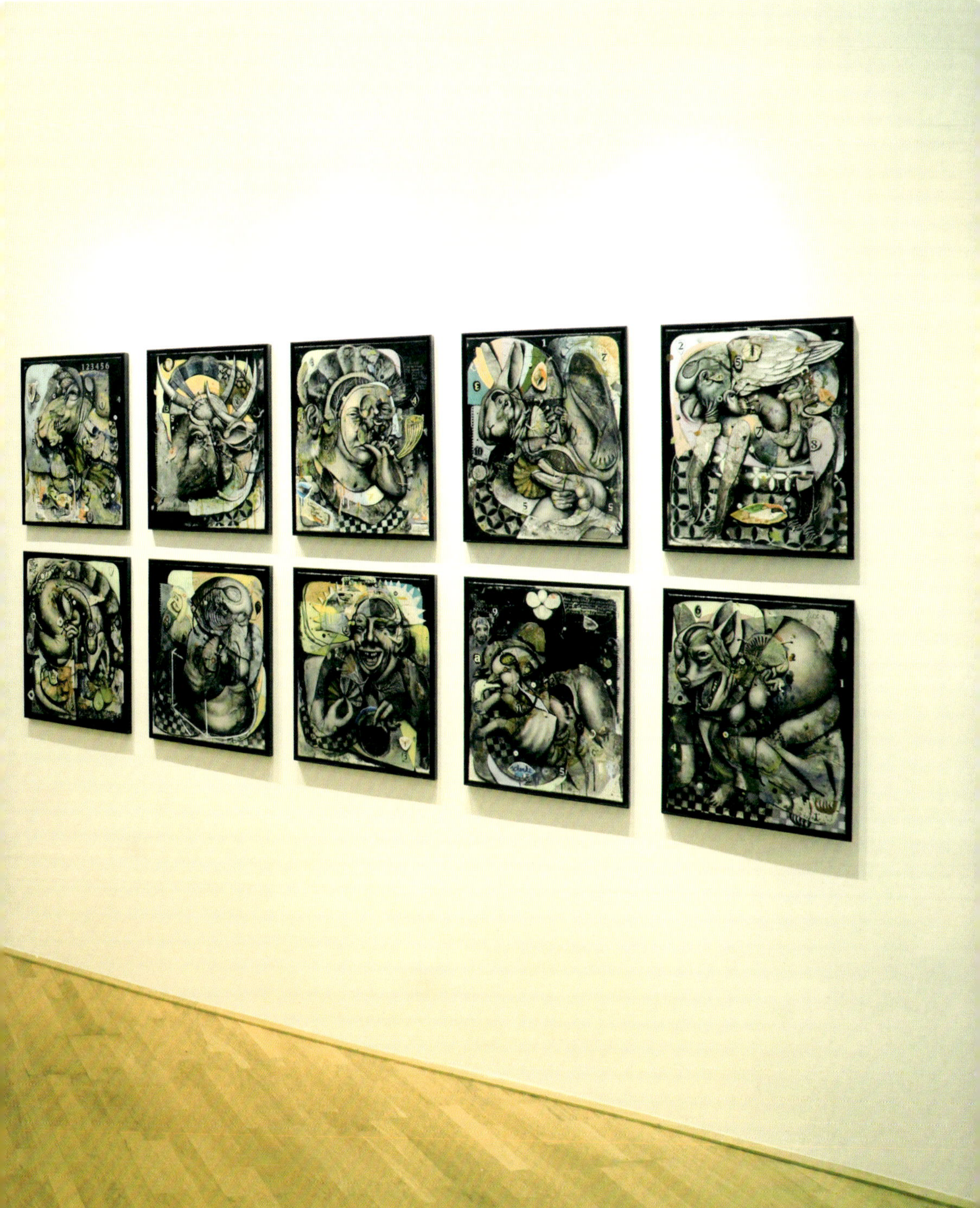

schlusskrebs | final crab

2019, Mixed Media on Canvas, 250 x 180 cm
Privatsammlung Österreich | Private Collection Austria

Vorherige Seite | Previous Page

Soloshow, »sirius«,
Galerie Felix Höller, Wien, Austria, 2019

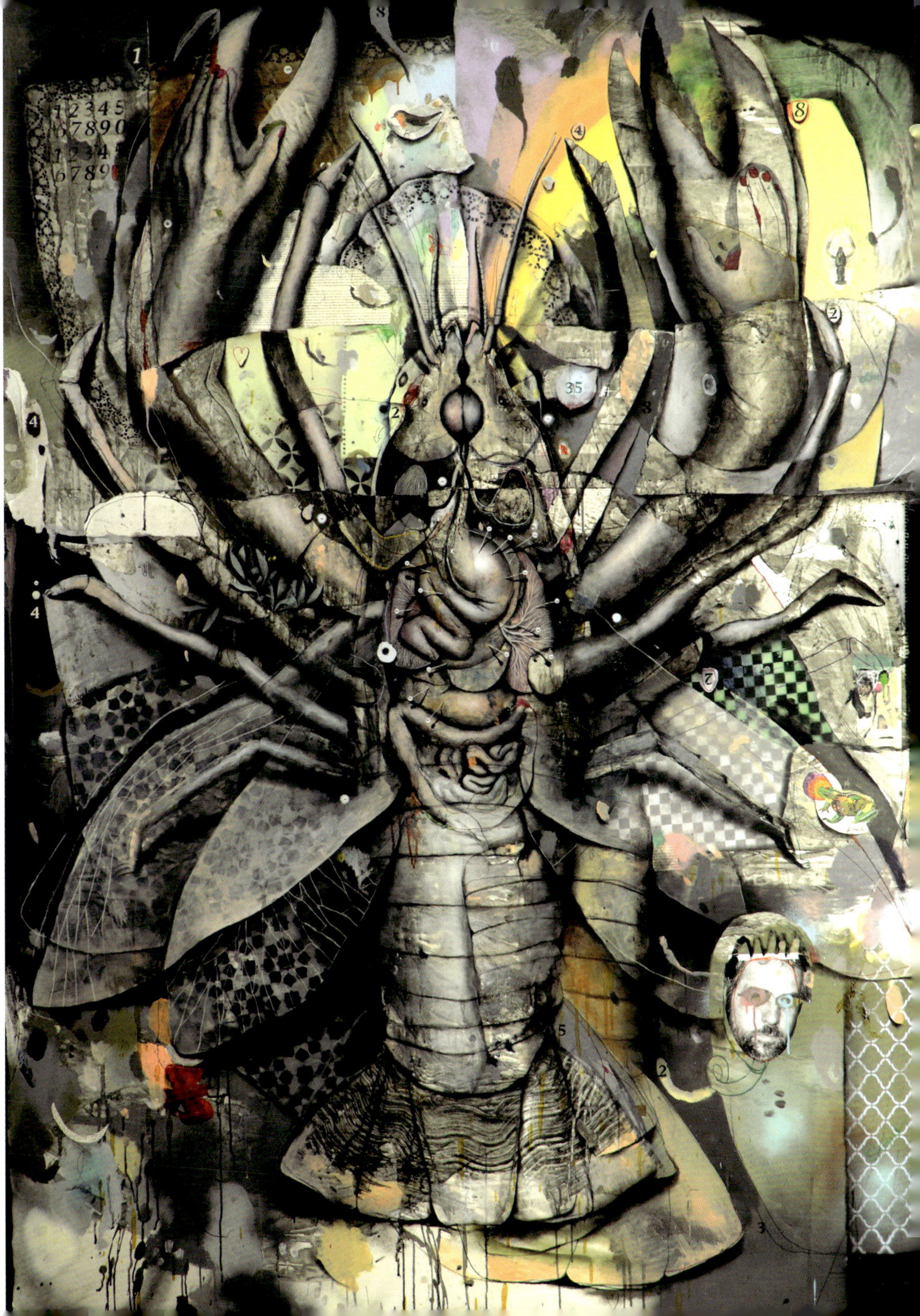

m analysiserer | m analyzer

2019, Mixed Media on Canvas, 40 x 30 cm
Privatsammlung Deutschland | Private Collection Germany

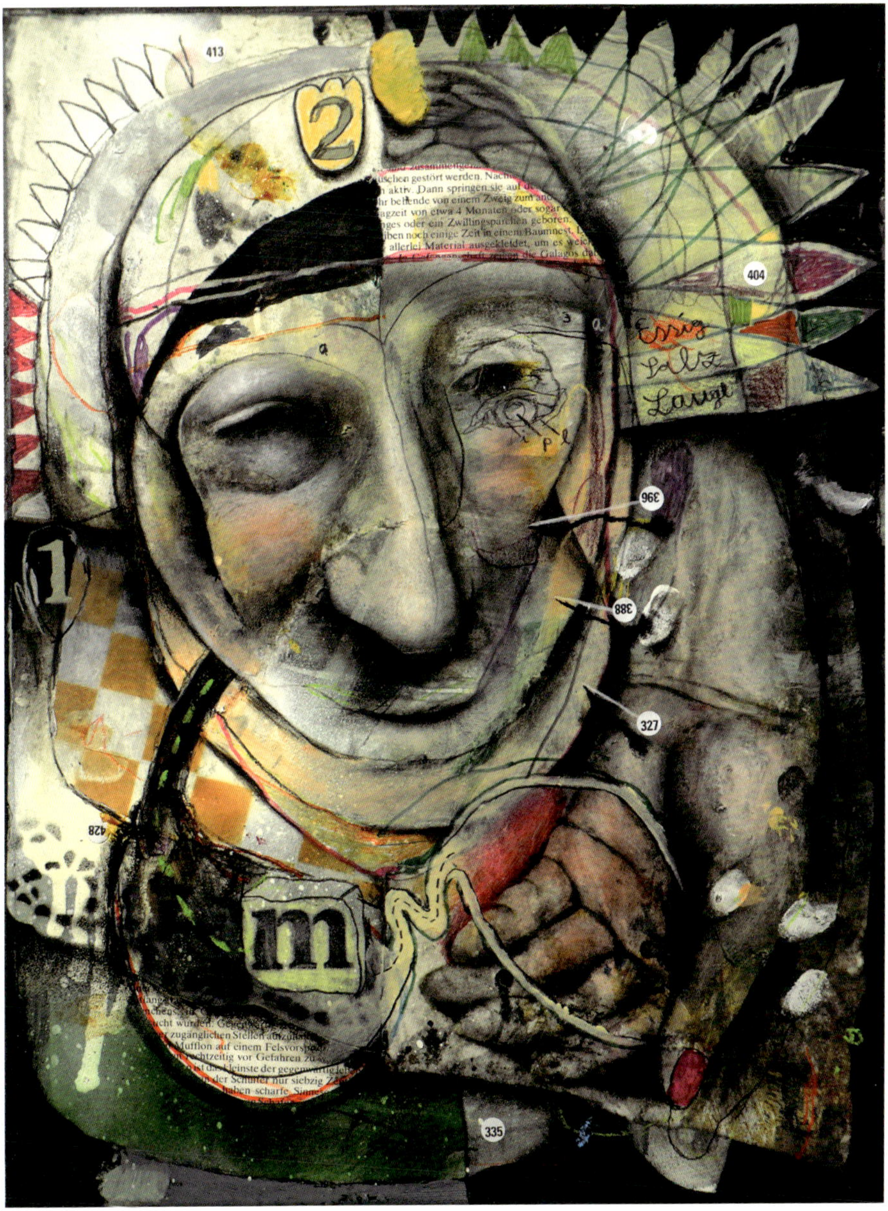
413
2
404
Essig
Salz
Lauge
396
1
388
327
428
m
335

fucks

2019, Mixed Media on Canvas, 60 x 50 cm
Privatsammlung Österreich | Private Collection Austria

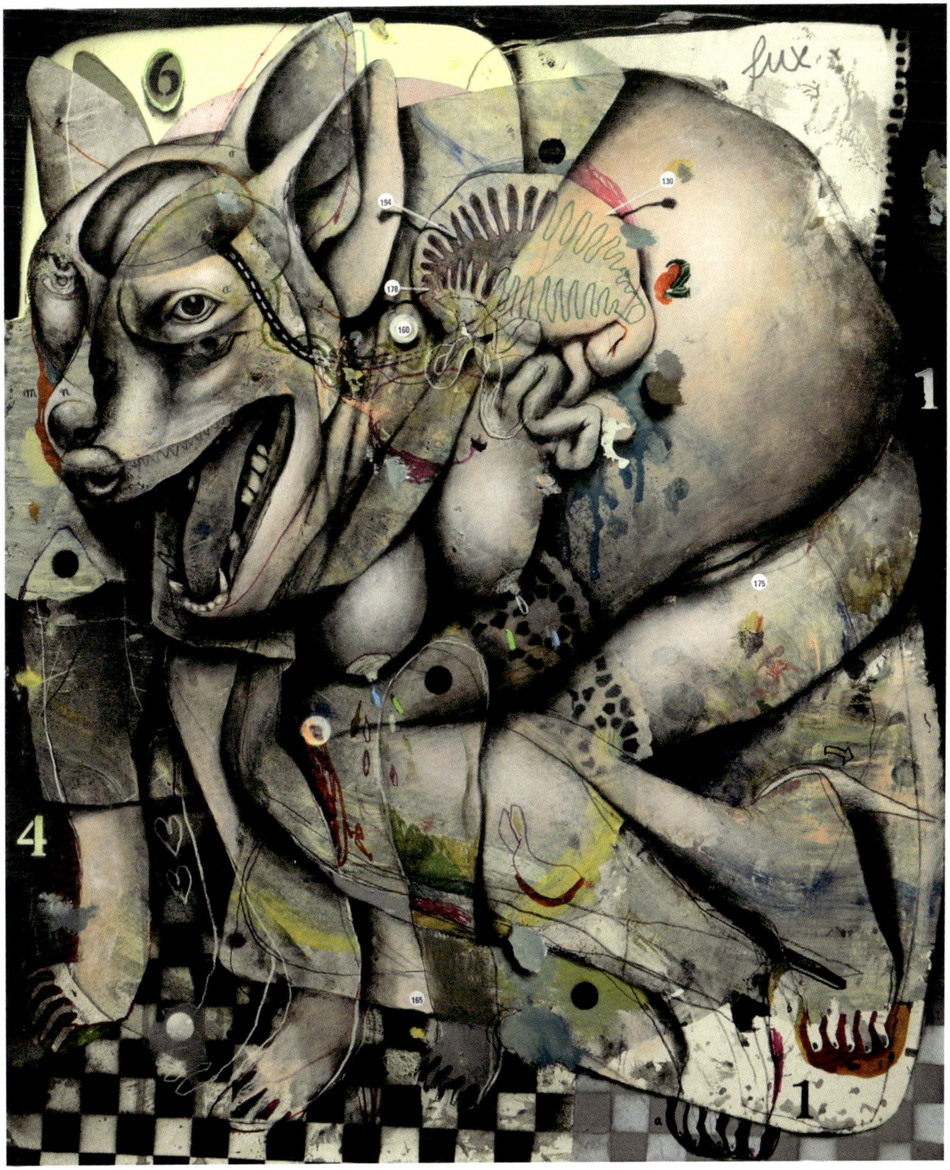

safthase (hätt ich mich doch besser versteckt) | juice rabbit (I should have hidden better)

2019, Mixed Media on Canvas, 60 x 50 cm
Privatsammlung Österreich | Private Collection Austria

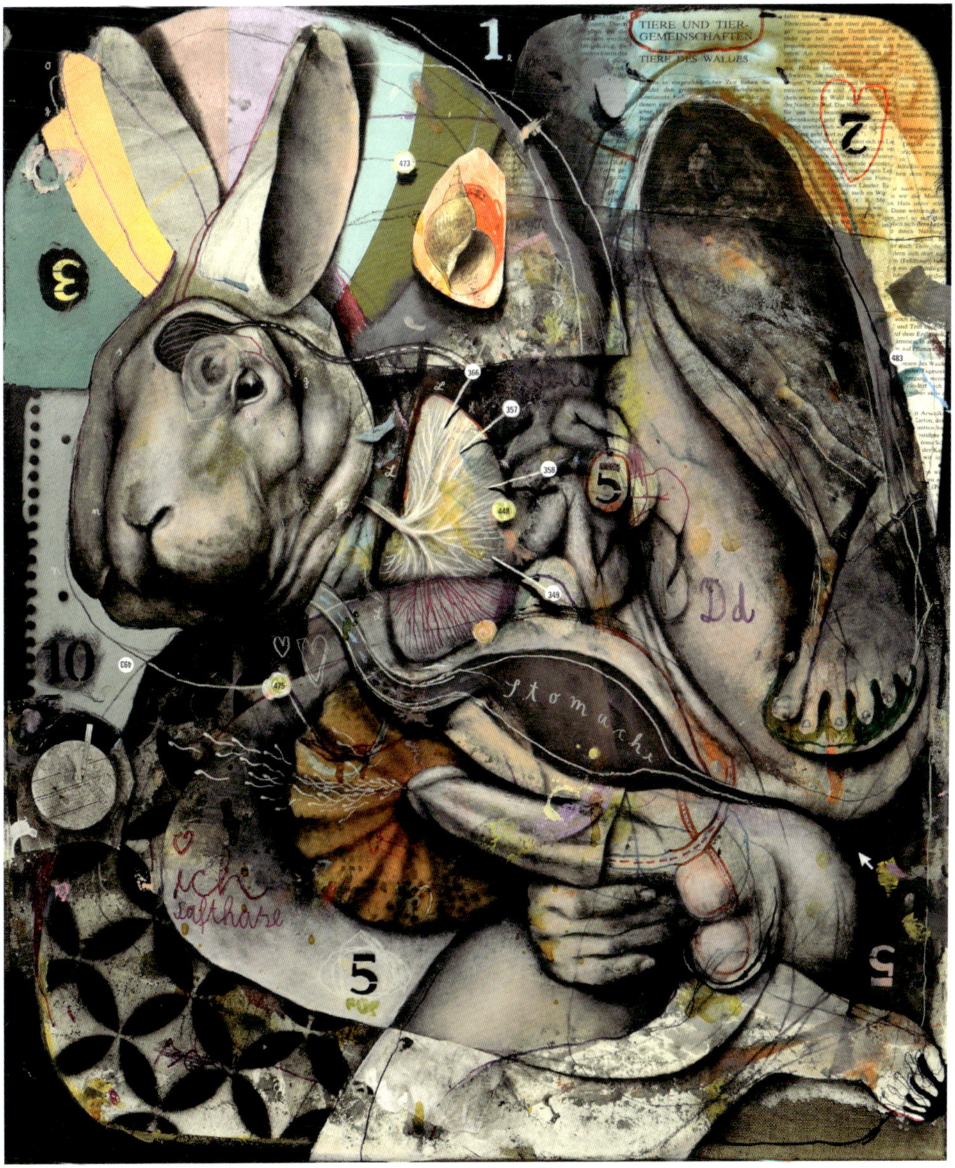
1
TIERE UND TIER-
GEMEINSCHAFTEN
TIERE DES WALDES
Dd
stomache
10
ich
5

schupfnudeltaube | potato noodle dove

2019, Mixed Media on Canvas, 60 x 50 cm
Privatsammlung Miami, USA | Private Collection Miami, USA

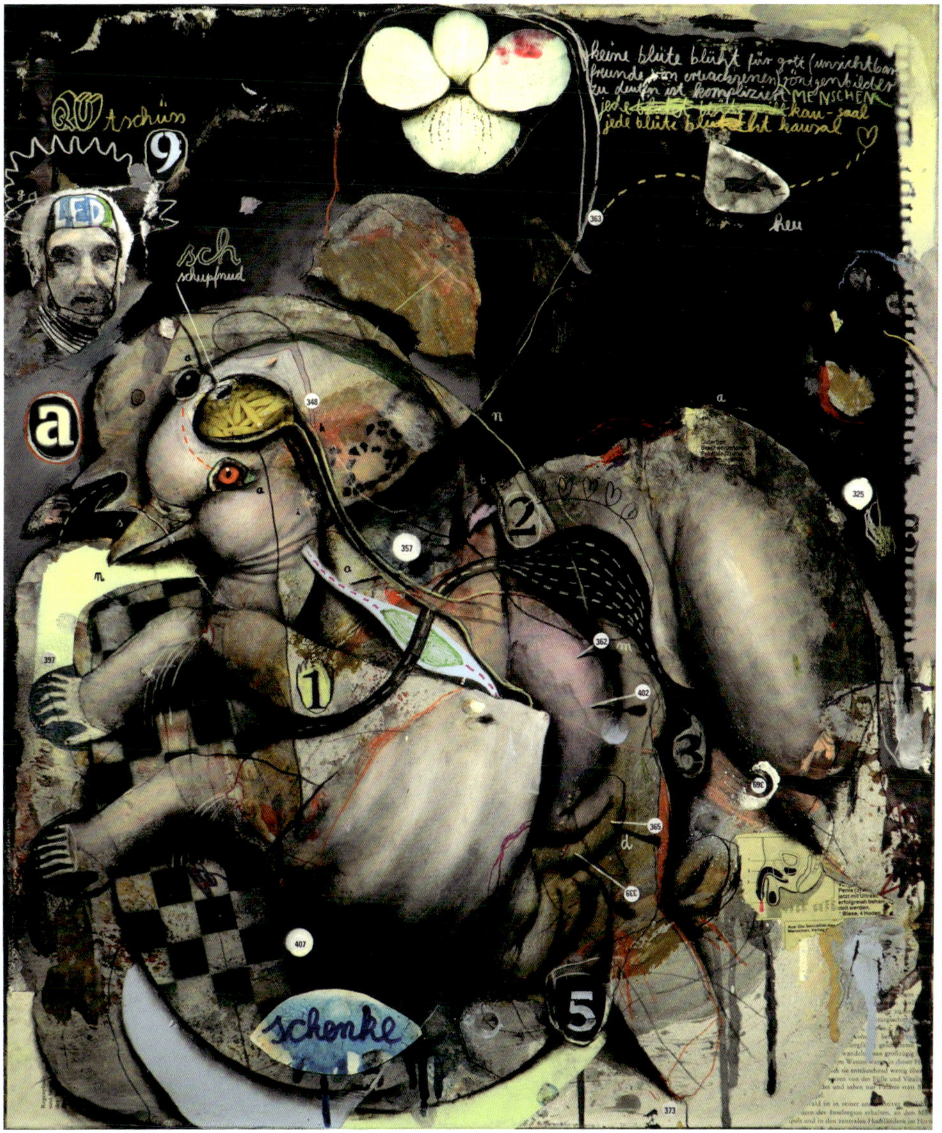
keine blüte blüht für gott
tschüss
sch
schenke
MENSCHEN
jede blüte blüht kausal

karlsruher tellerpferd | karlsruhe plate horse

2019, Mixed Media on Canvas, 100 x 80 cm
Privatsammlung Deutschland | Private Collection Germany

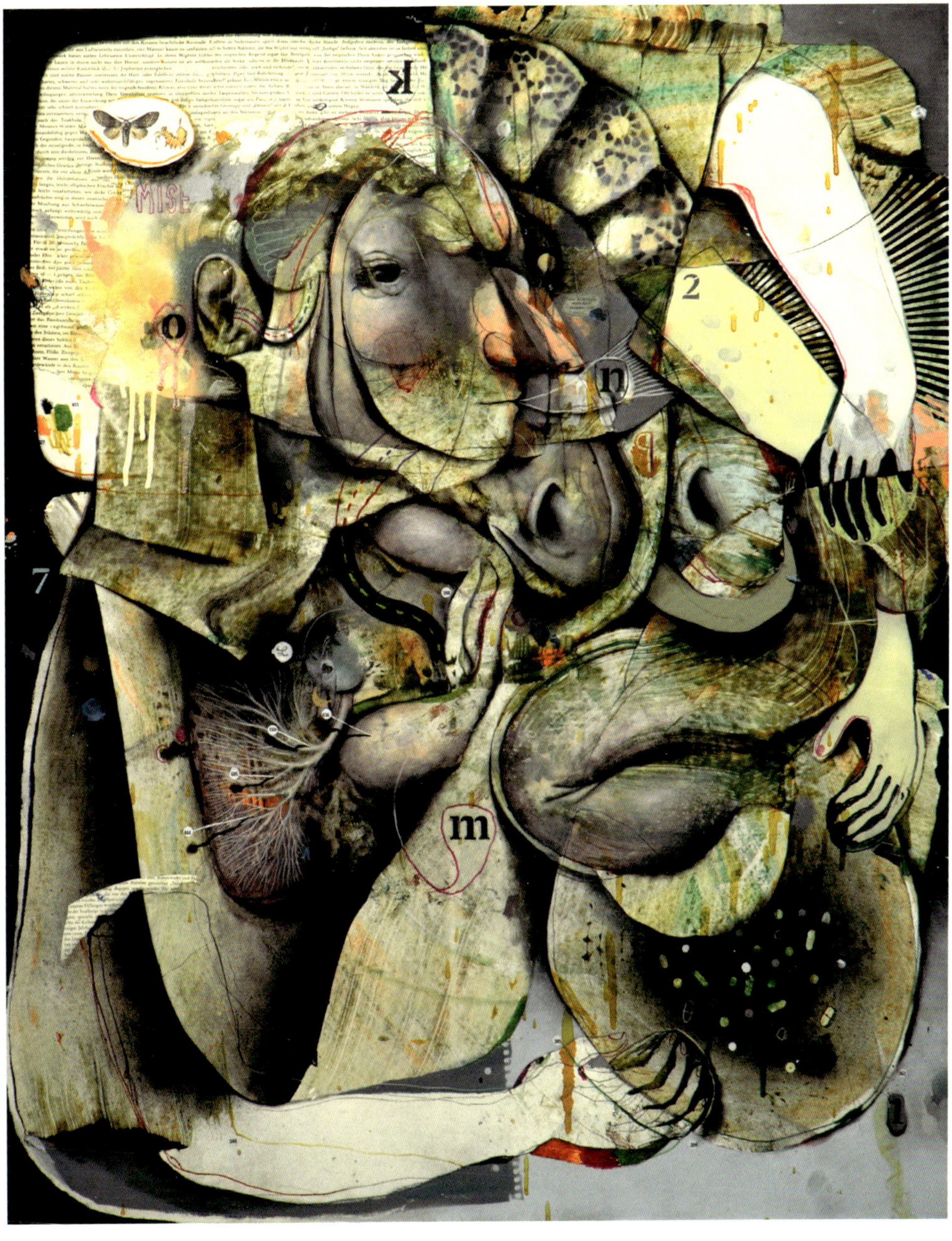
MISE
o
n
2
7
m

erkenntnis im plastiksessel | perception in the plastic armchair

2019, Mixed Media on Canvas, 140 x 130 cm

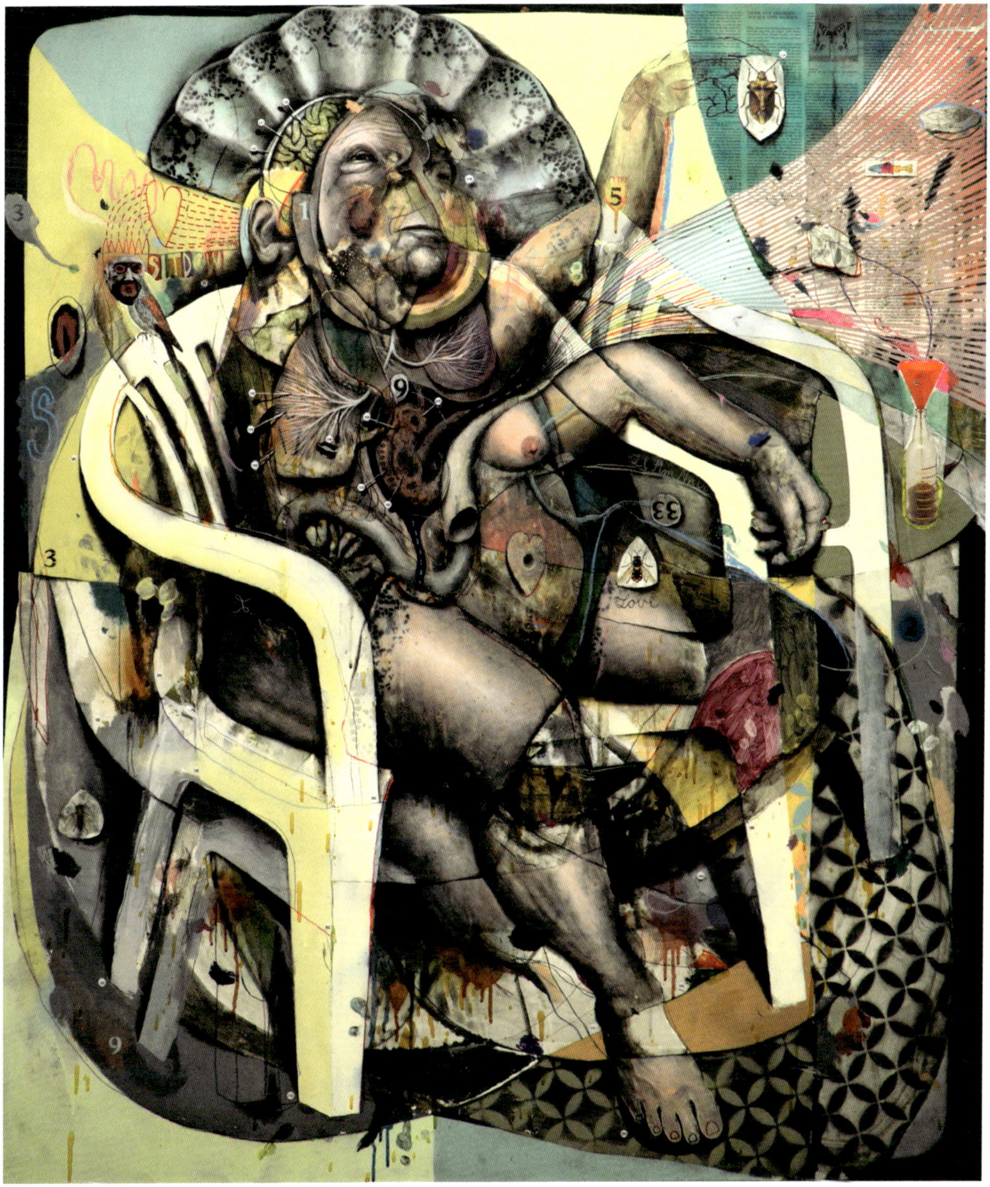

selbstschnürer (glücklich) | self lacer (happy)

2019, Mixed Media on Canvas, 140 x 90 cm
Privatsammlung Israel | Private Collection Israel

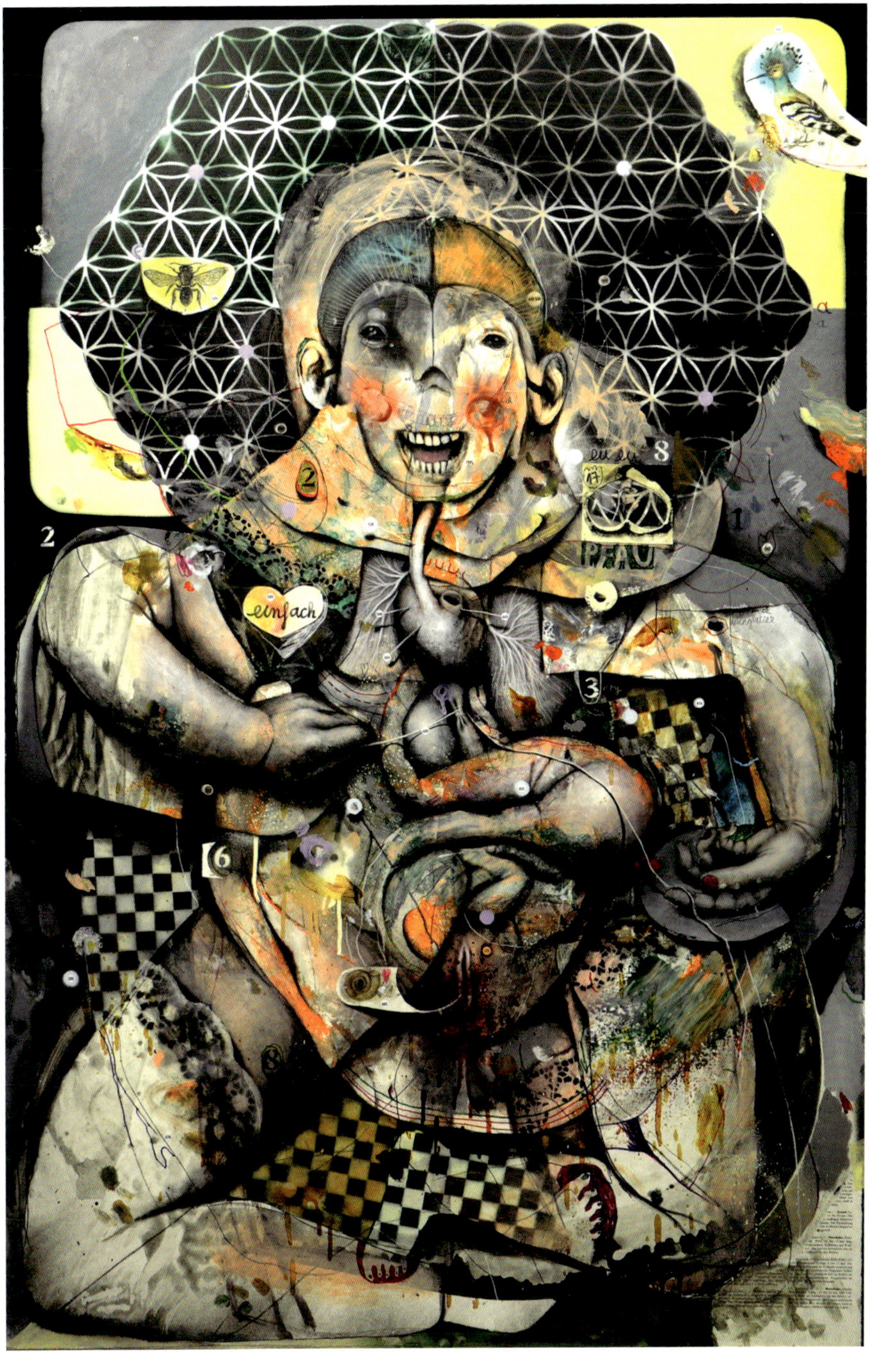
einfach

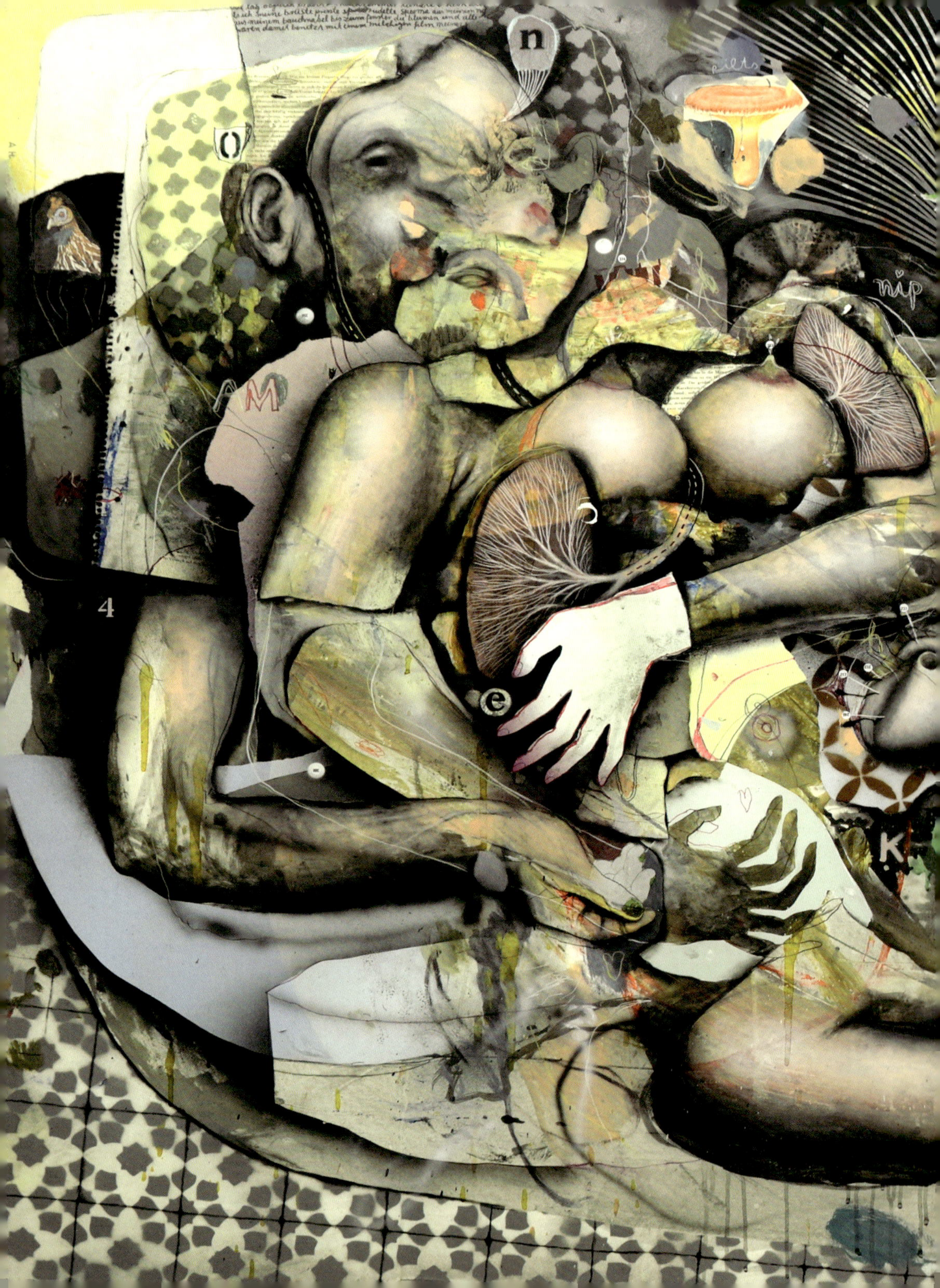

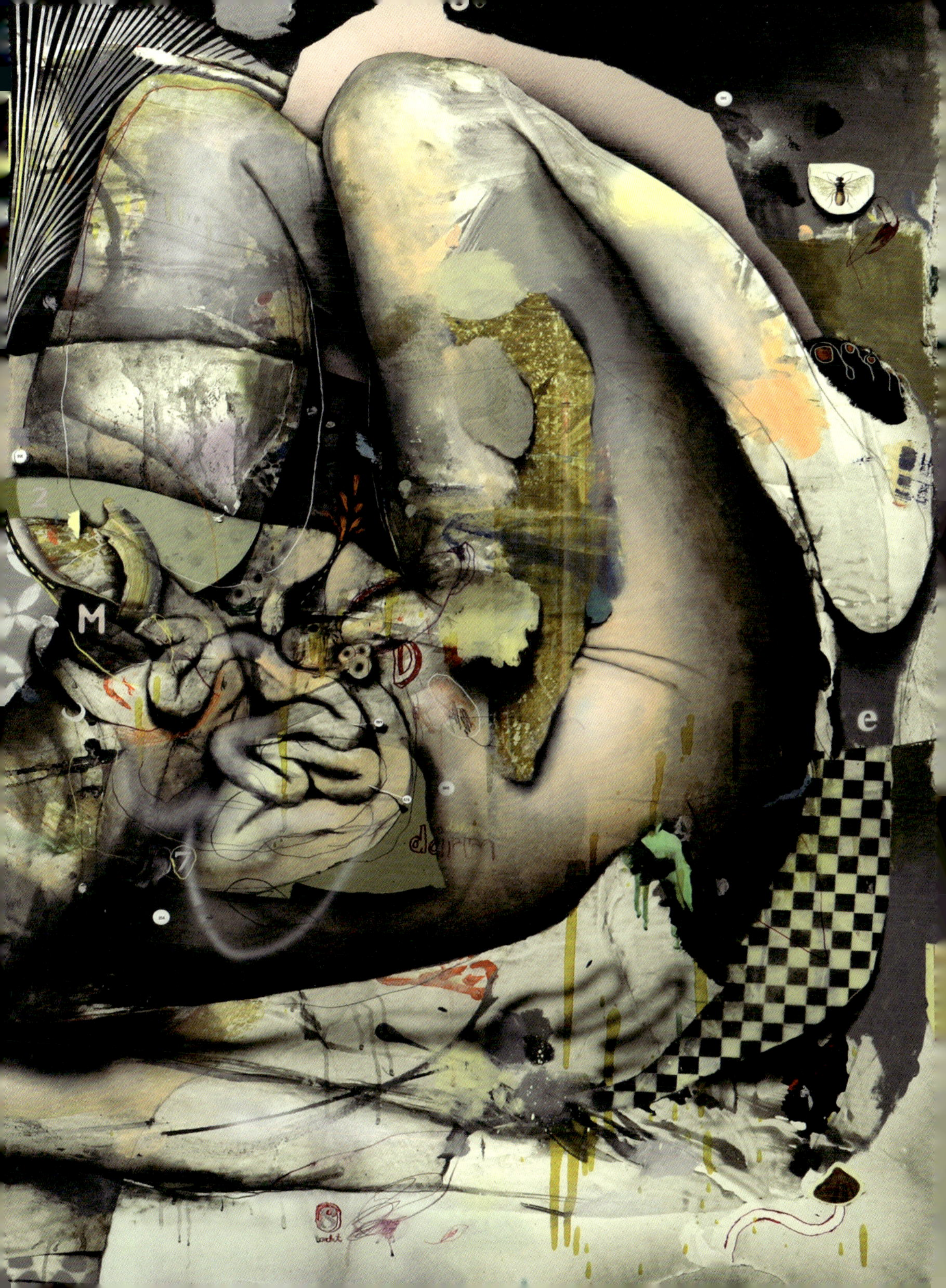

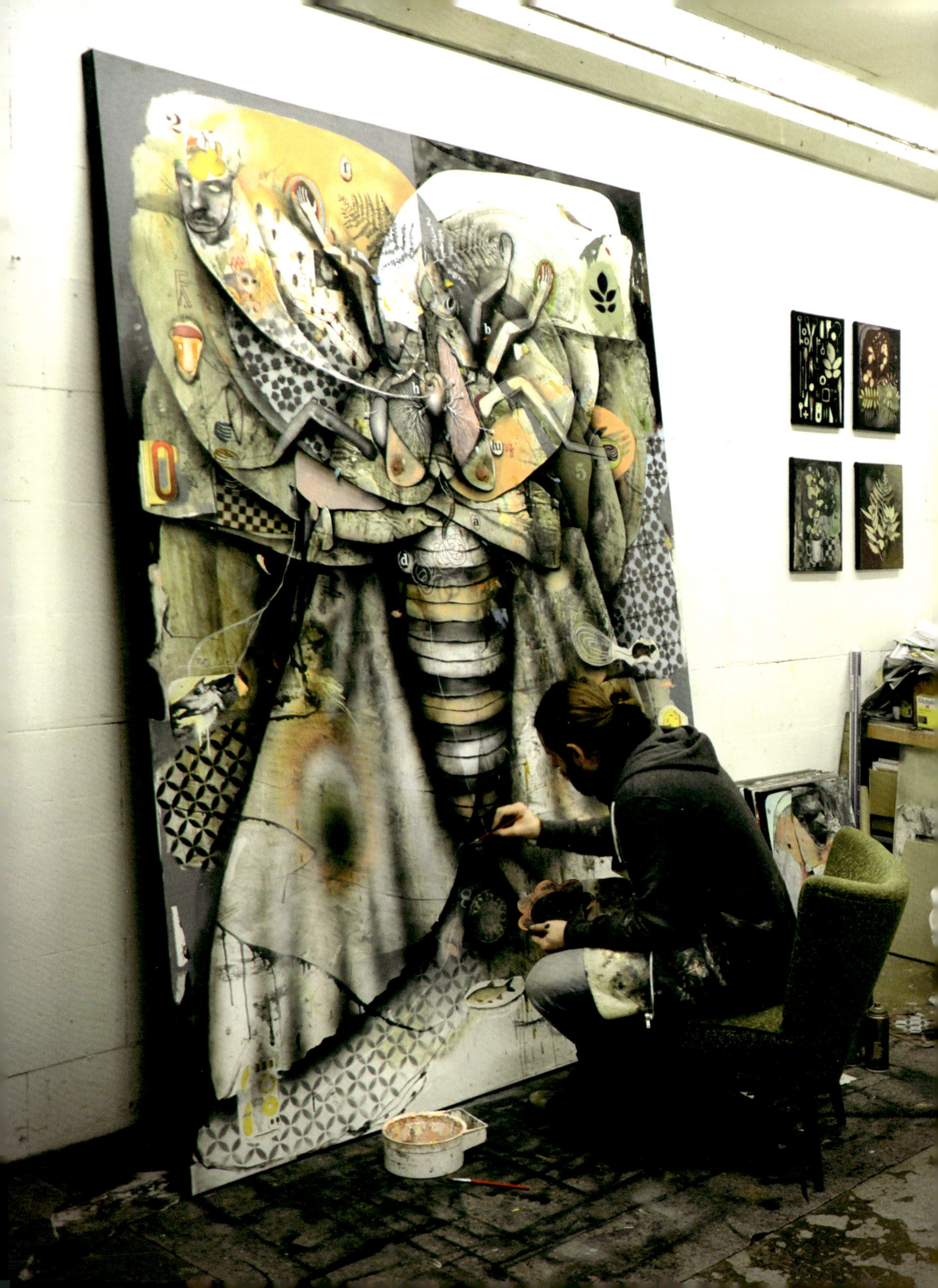

flotte motte | racy moth

2019, Mixed Media on Canvas, 250 x 170 cm
Privatsammlung Deutschland | Private Collection Germany
Foto: Studio Karlsruhe, Germany, 2019

Vorherige Seite | Previous Page

nachdenklicher akt mit specknabelfontäne | reflective nude with blubber navel fountain

2019, Mixed Media on Canvas, 140 x 200 cm
Privatsammlung Deutschland | Private Collection Germany

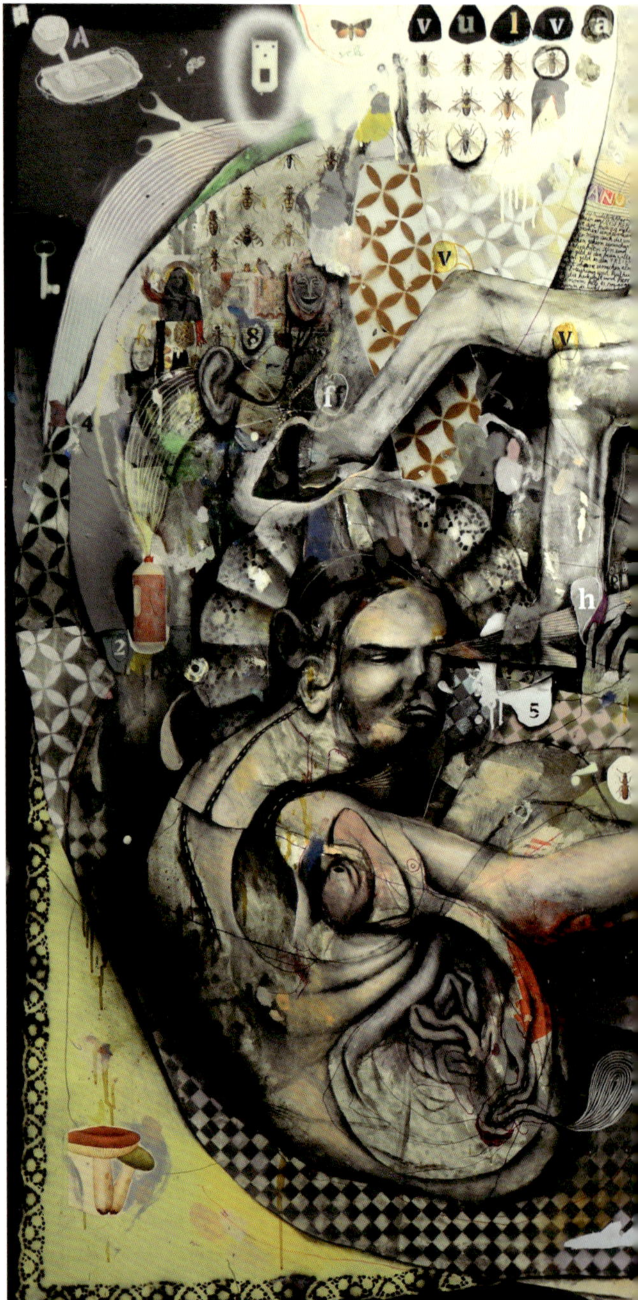

der sturz der froschkönigin

the fall of the frog queen

2019, Mixed Media on Canvas, 180 x 250 cm
Privatsammlung Österreich | Private Collection Austria

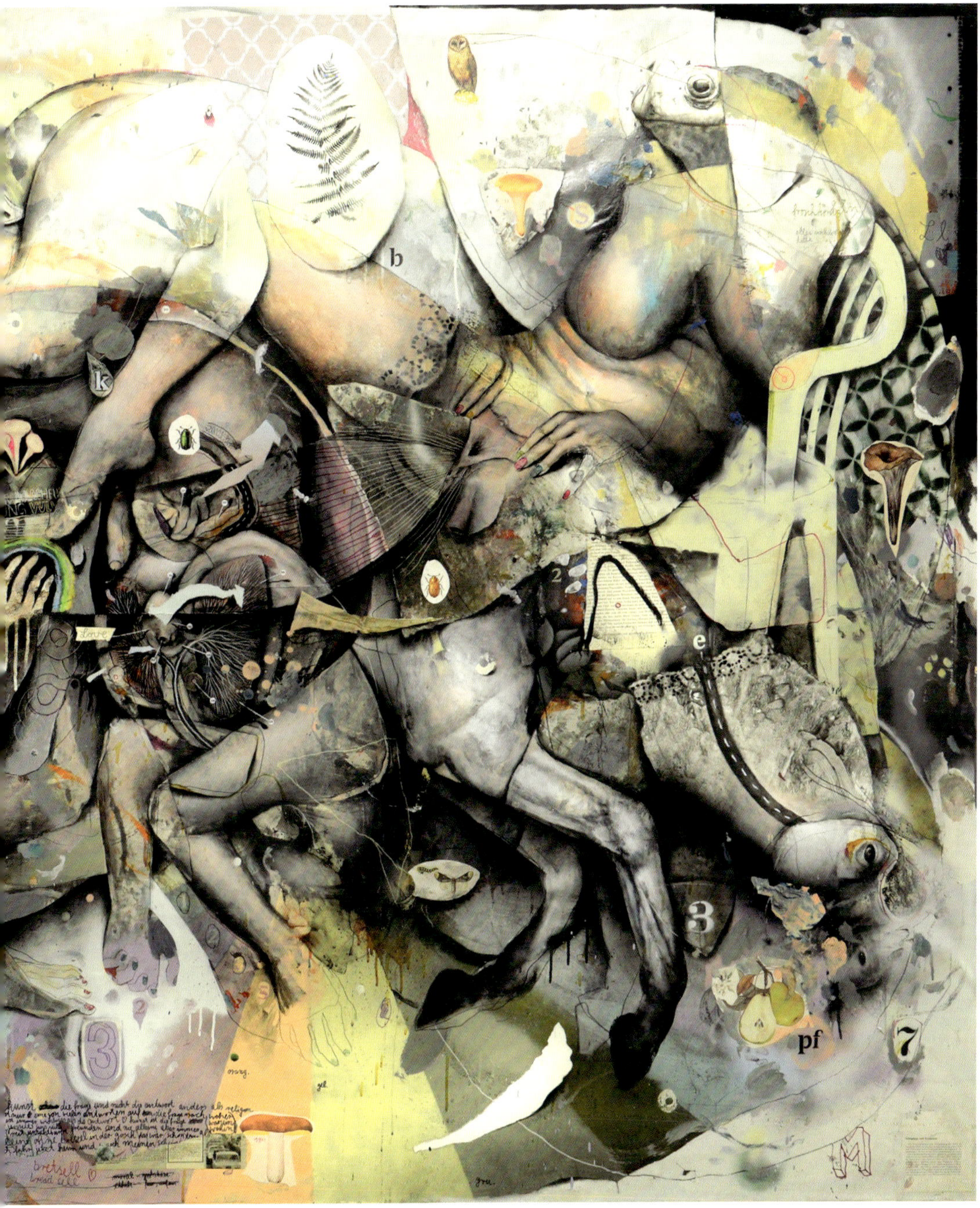

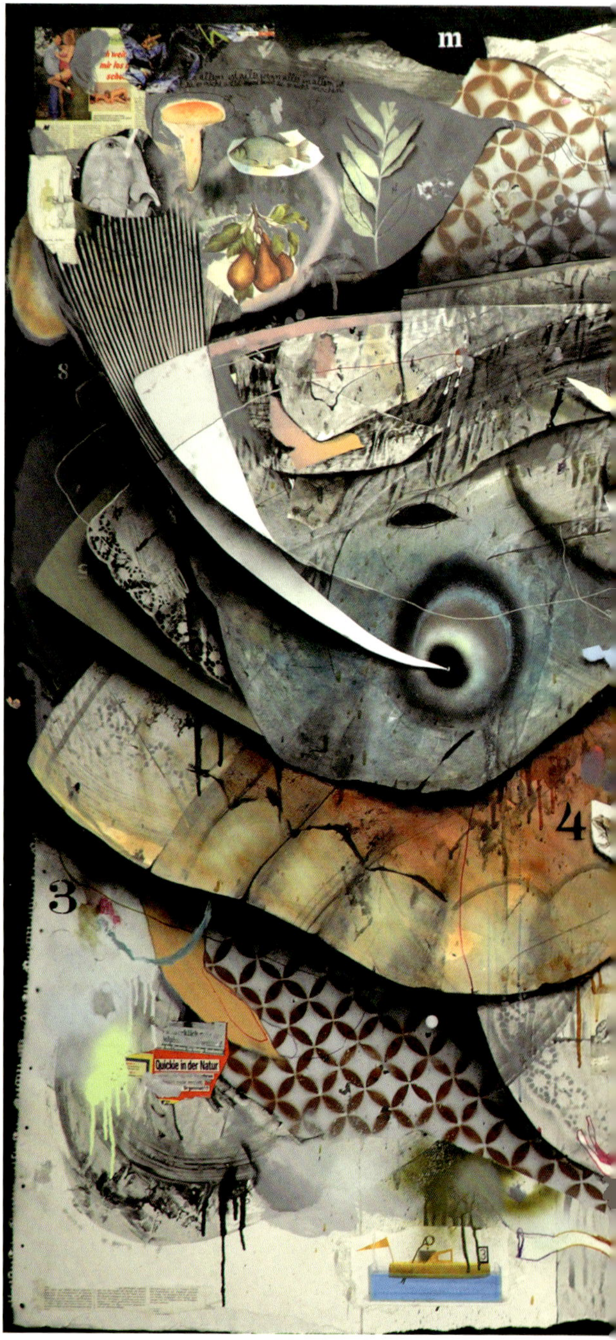

alter falter | old moth

2019, Mixed Media on Canvas, 180 x 250 cm
Privatsammlung Deutschland | Private Collection Germany

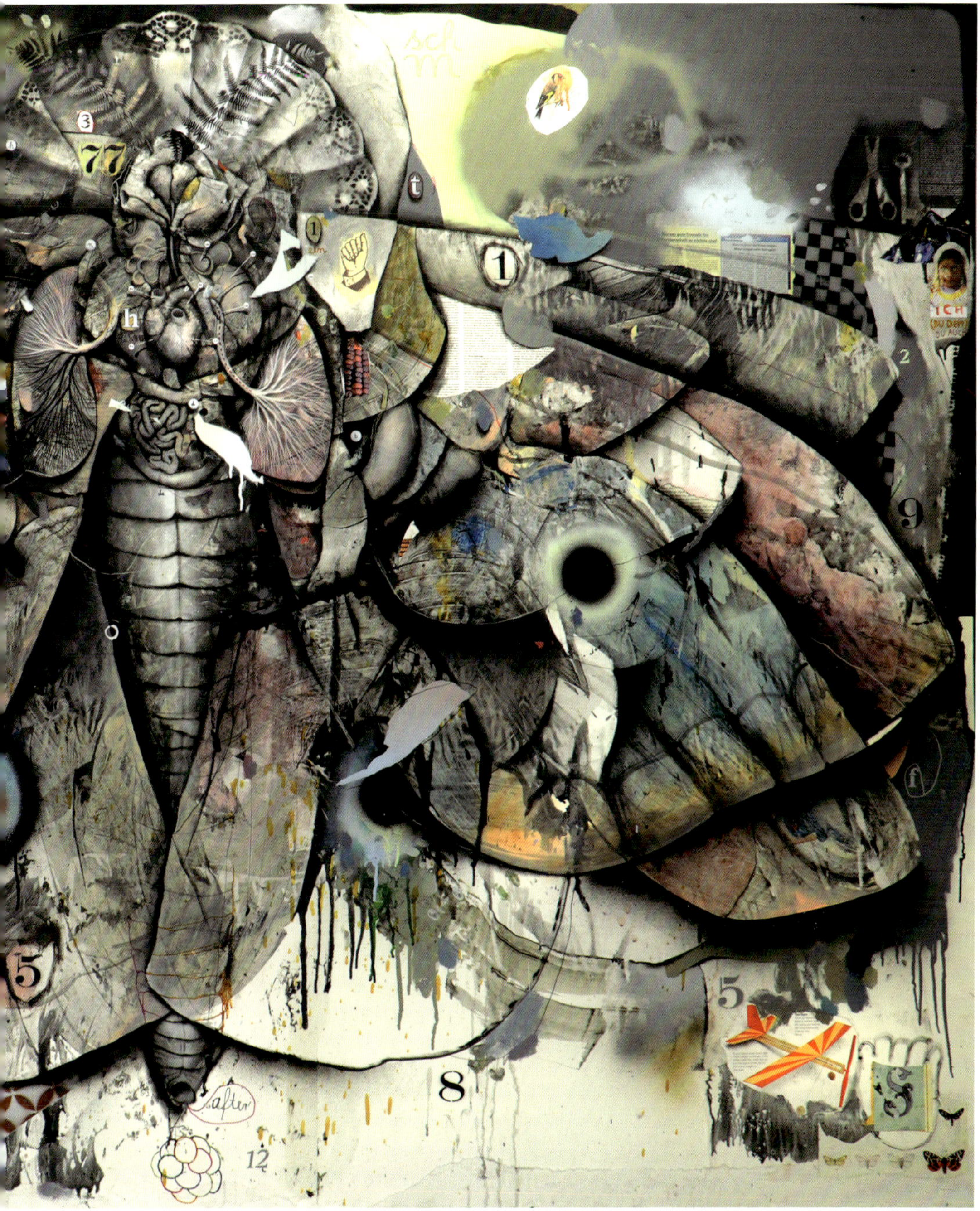

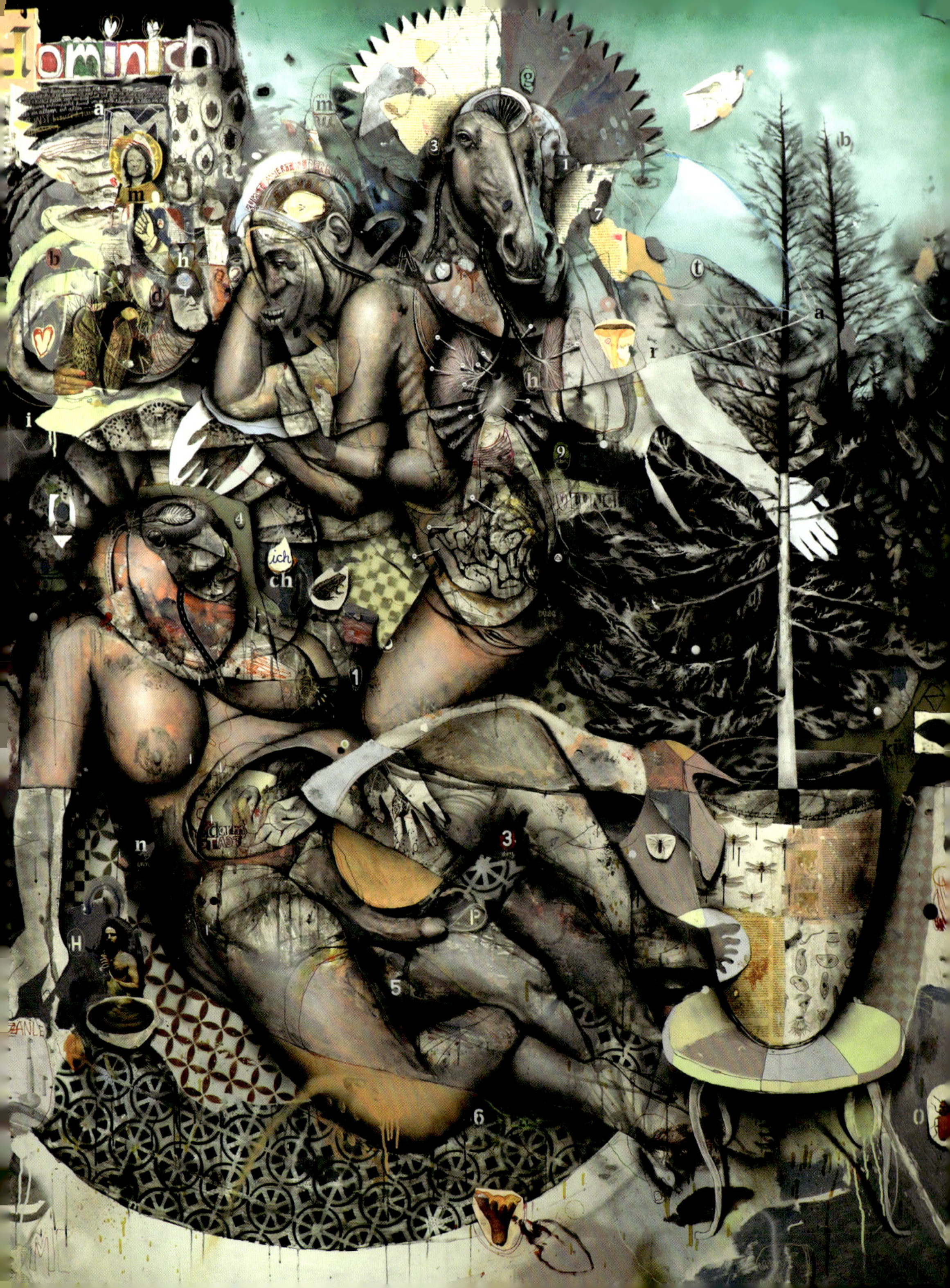
ich
ch

status quo vadis in veritas ananas

2019, Mixed Media on Canvas, 250 x 200 cm

mischa

2020, Mixed Media on Canvas, 40 x 30 cm
Privatsammlung Deutschland | Private Collection Germany

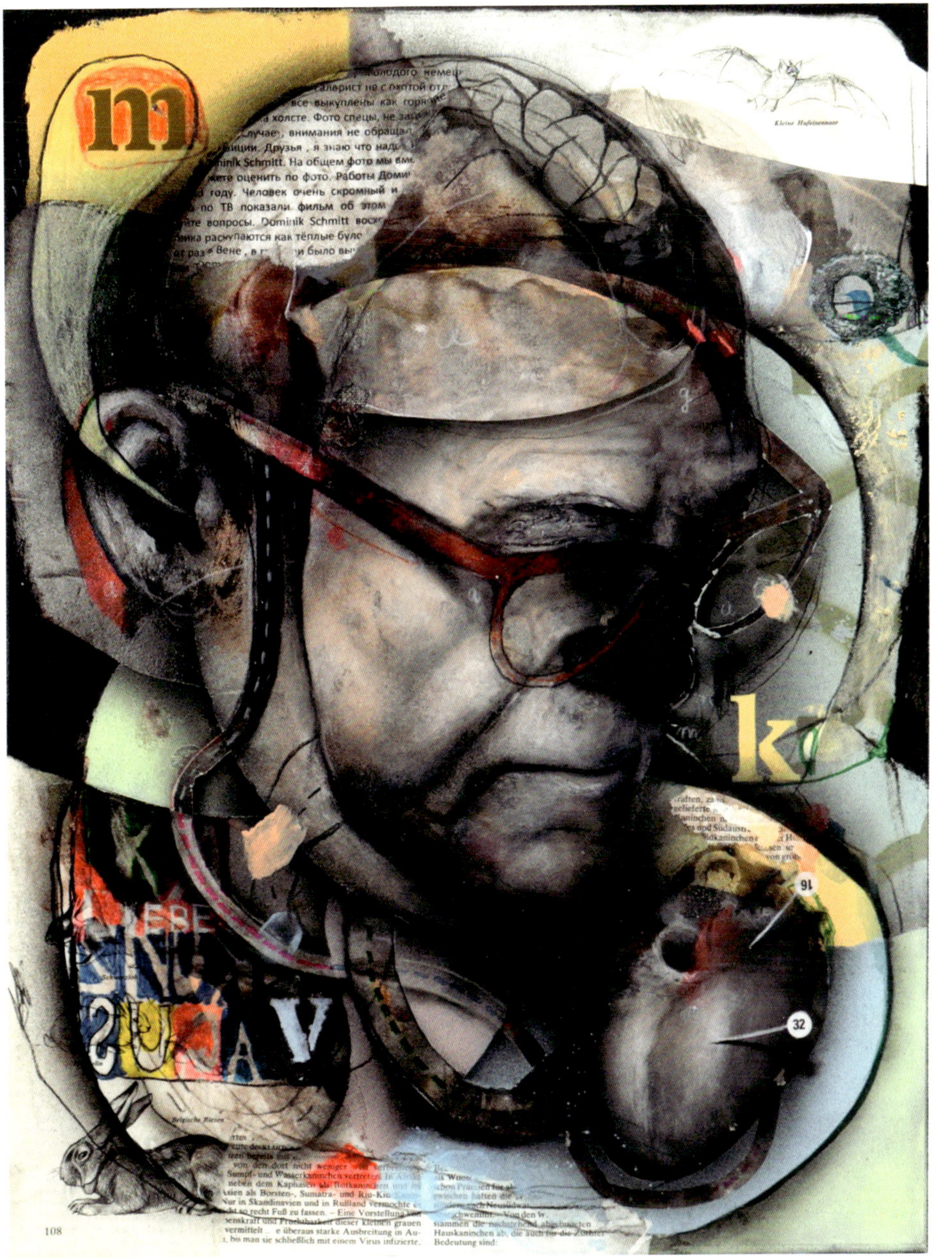

57

2020, Mixed Media on Canvas, 60 x 50 cm
Privatsammlung Österreich | Private Collection Austria

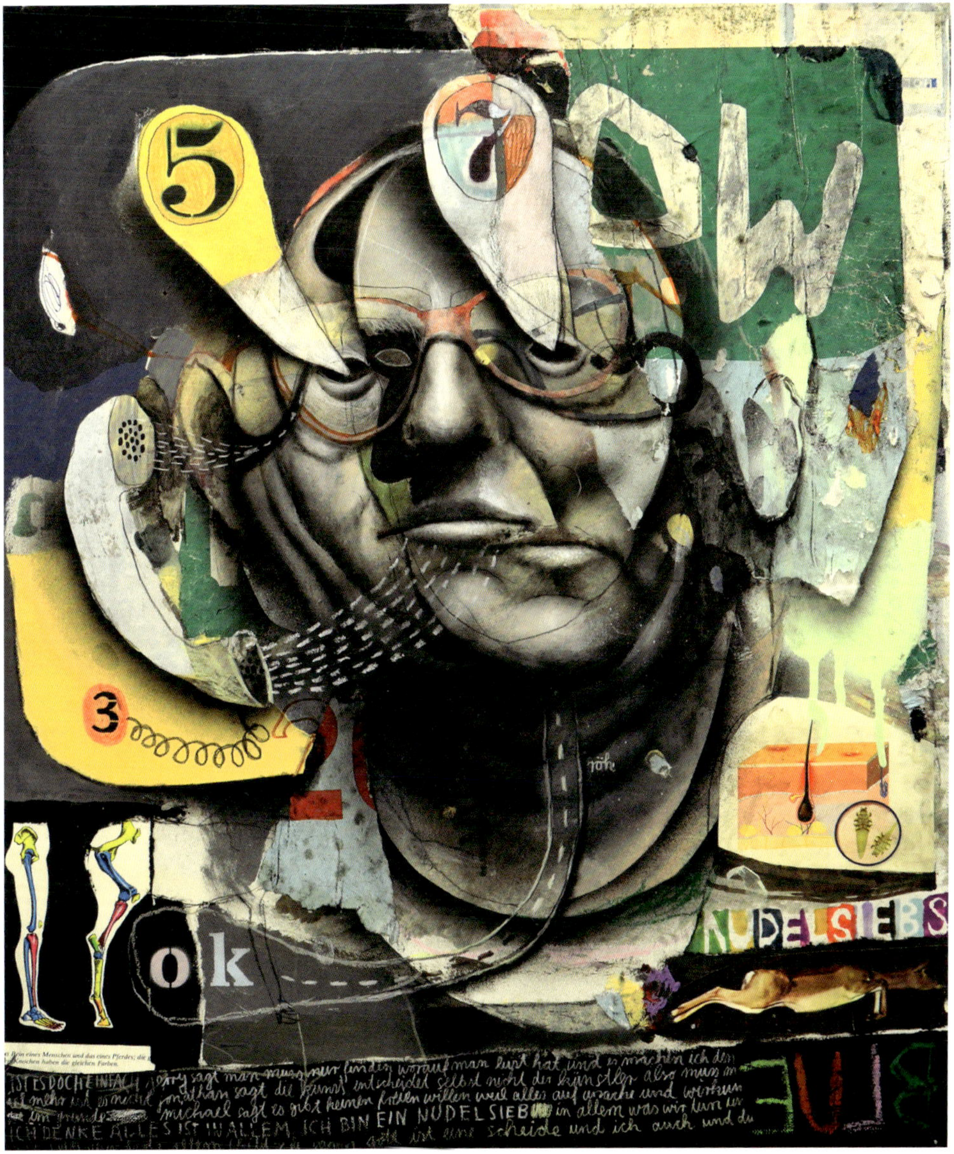
5
3
ok
NUDELSIEBS
BLUE
Knochen haben die gleichen Farben.
ISTESDOCHEINFACH
jonathan sagt die kunst entscheidet selbst nicht der künstler
michael sagt es gibt keinen freien willen weil alles auf ursache und wirkun
ICH BIN EIN NUDELSIEB
ICH DENKE ALLES IST IN ALLEM
scheide und ich auch und du

eastwood

2020, Mixed Media on Canvas, 60 x 50 cm
Privatsammlung Deutschland | Private Collection Germany

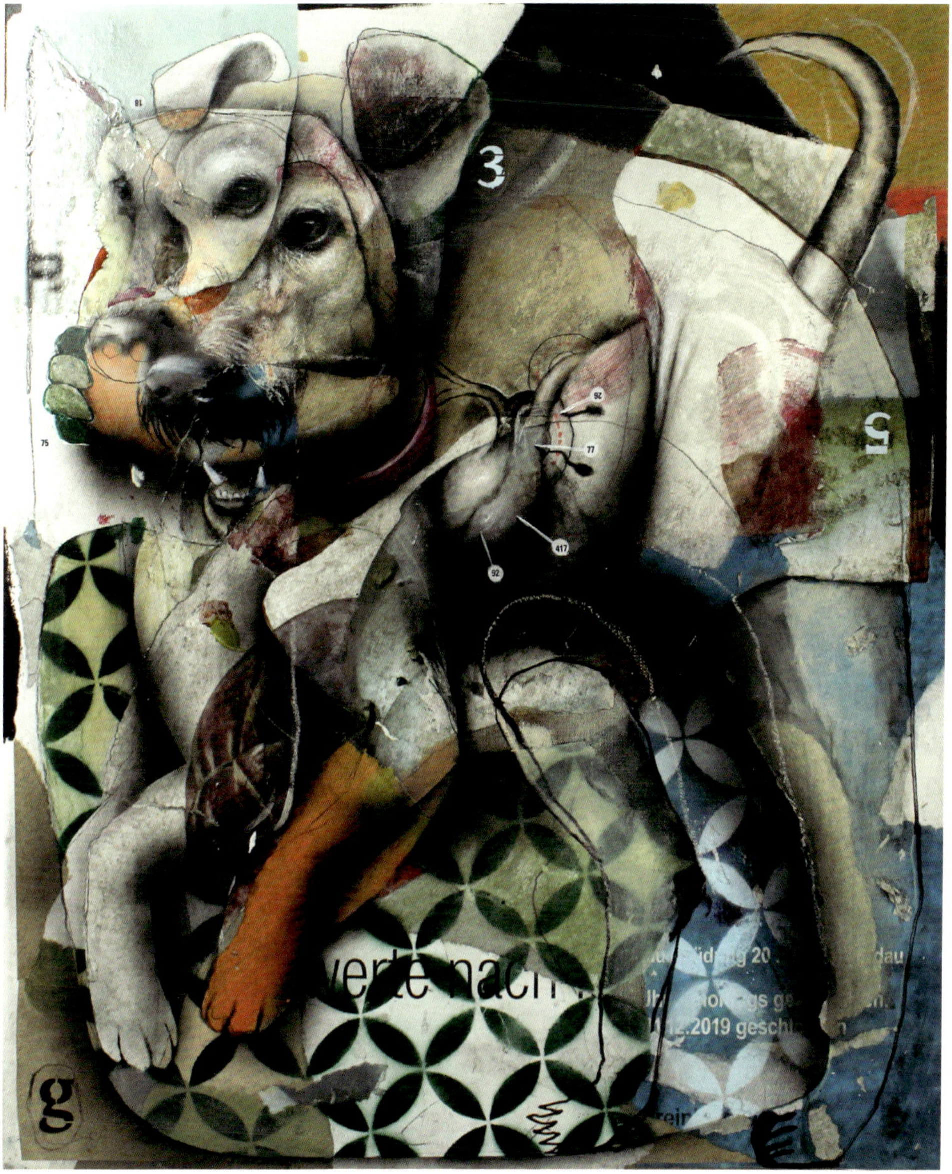

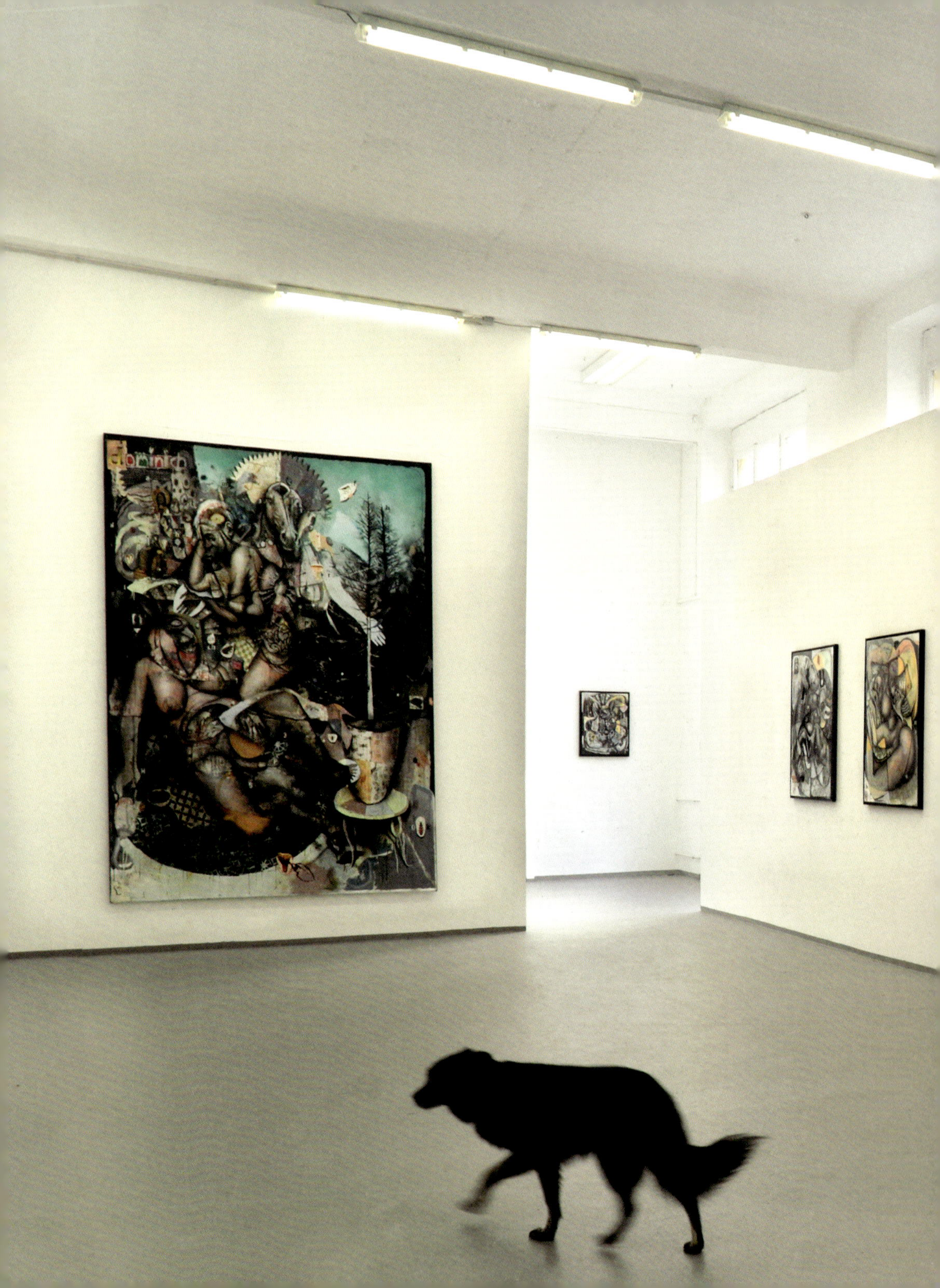

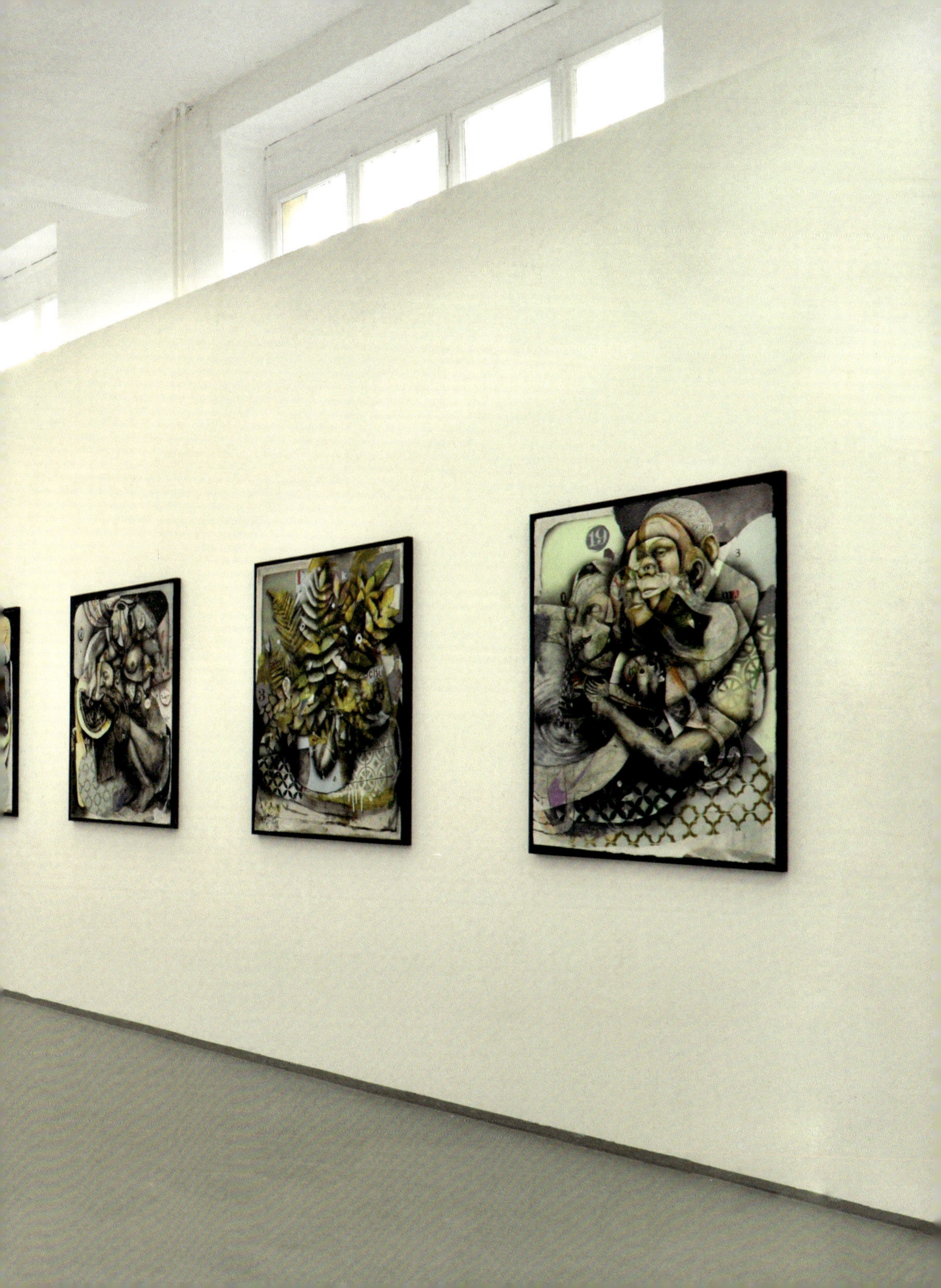

tante mit speiseeis | auntie with ice cream

2020, Mixed Media on Canvas, 60 x 50 cm
Privatsammlung Deutschland | Private Collection Germany

Vorherige Seite | Previous Page

Soloshow, »status quo vadis in veritas ananas«,
Galerie Thomas Hühsam, Offenbach am Main, Germany, 2020

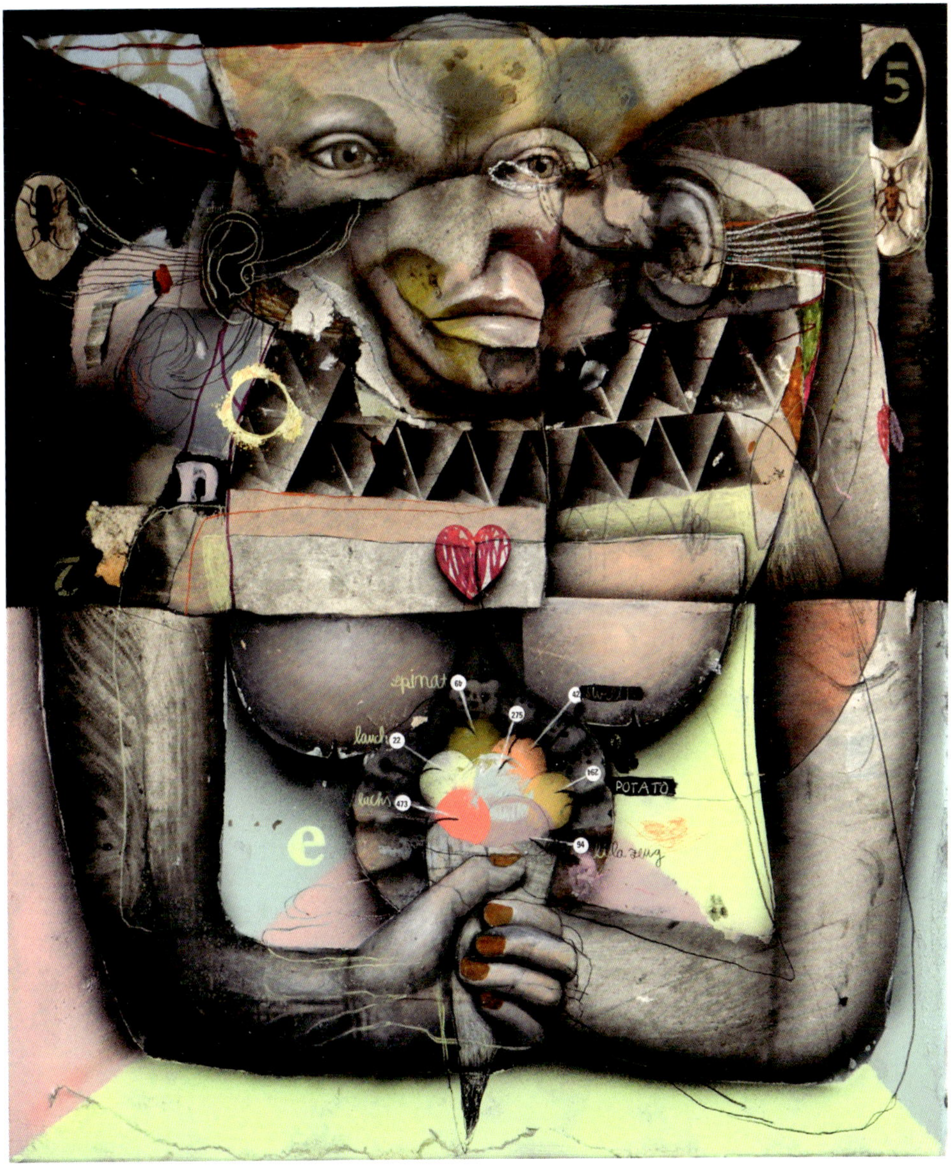
spinat
lauch
lachs
POTATO

handplansch for 30 seconds | handsplash for 30 seconds

2020, Mixed Media on Canvas, 100 x 80 cm

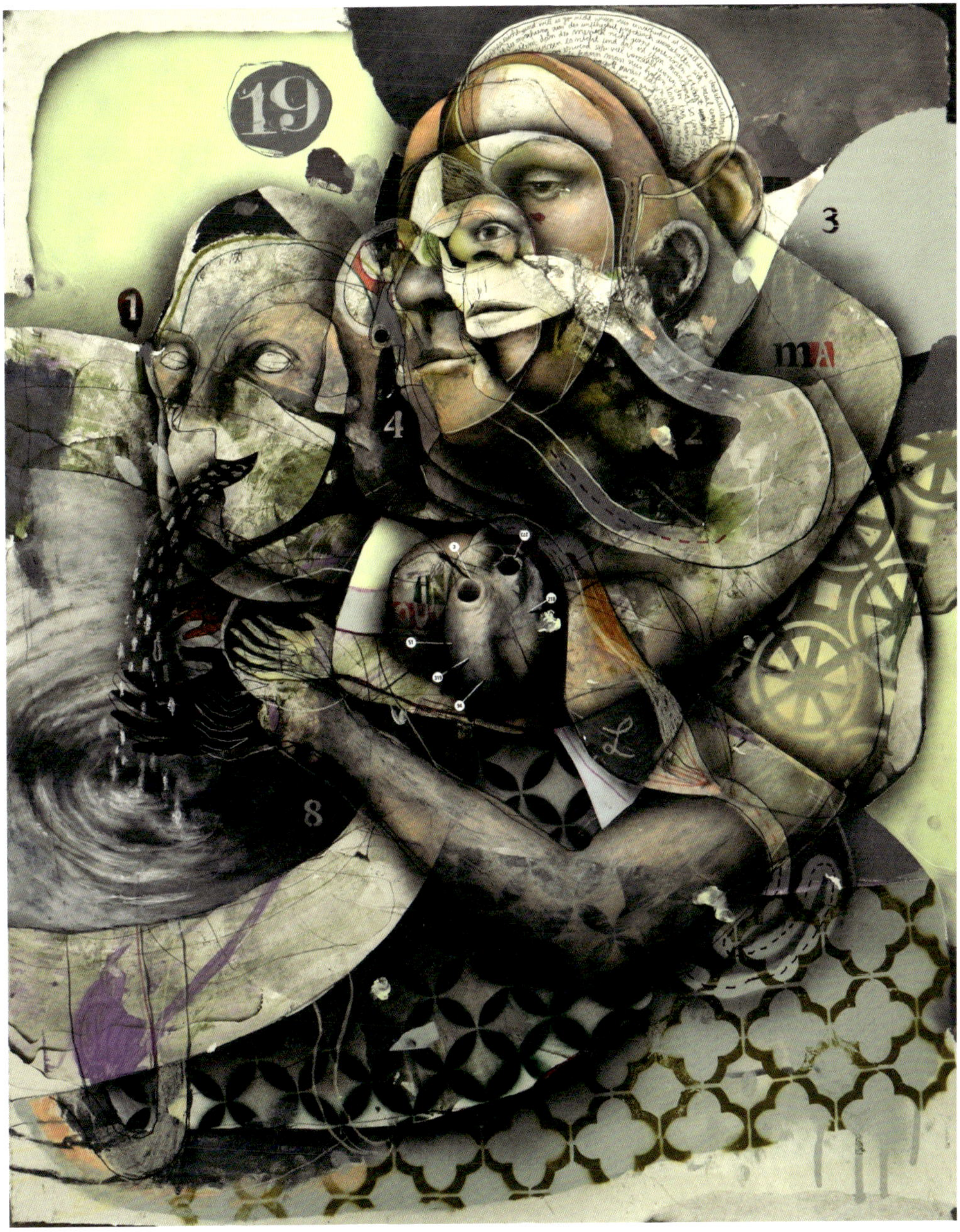
19
1
3
mA
4
8

ballongirl

2020, Mixed Media on Canvas, 100 x 80 cm
Privatsammlung Deutschland | Private Collection Germany

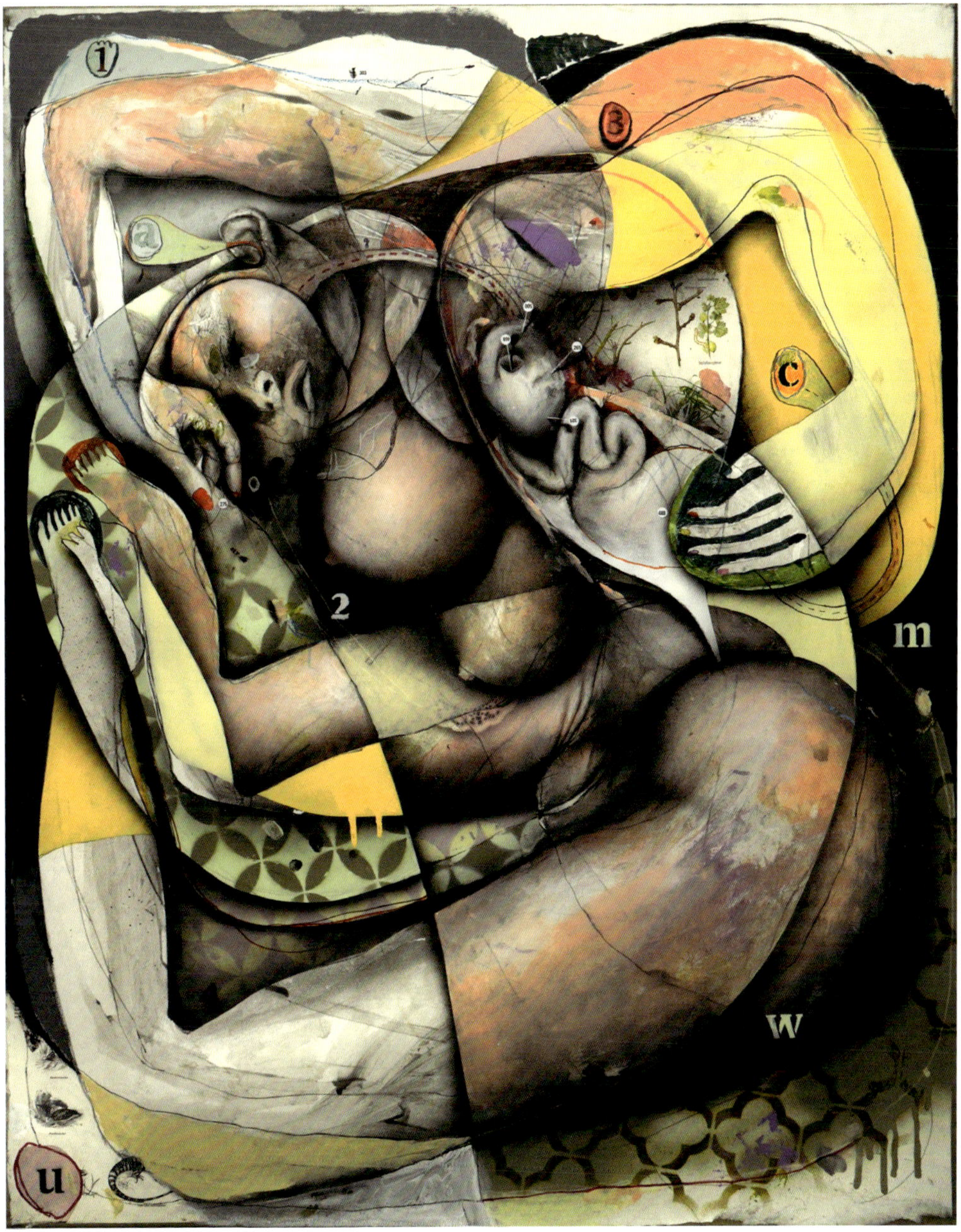

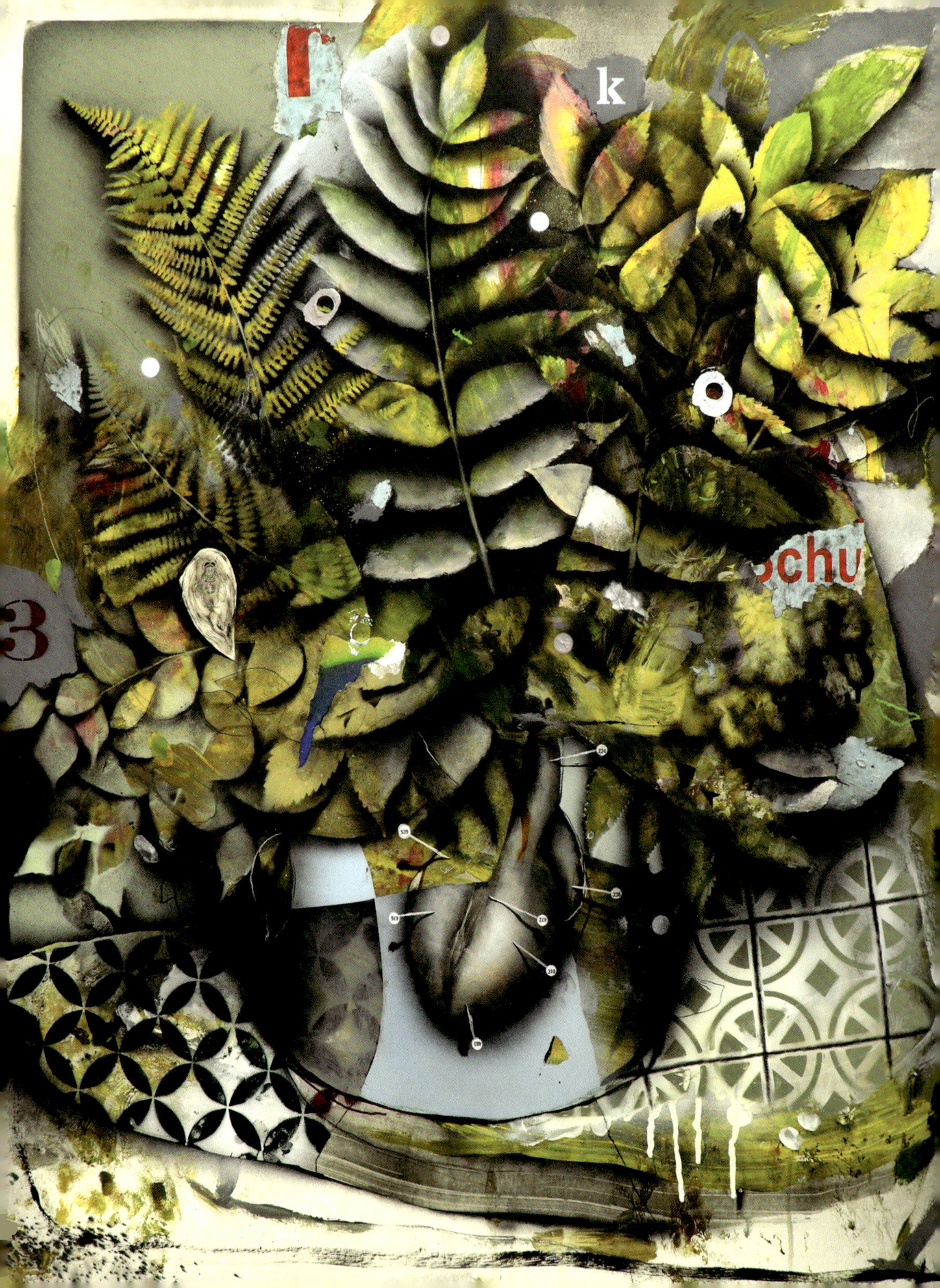
k
chu
3

bloomstrauß | bloom bouquet

2020, Mixed Media on Canvas, 100 x 80 cm
Privatsammlung Leipzig, Deutschland | Private Collection Leipzig, Germany

aufsitzer | rider

2020, Mixed Media on Canvas, 100 x 80 cm

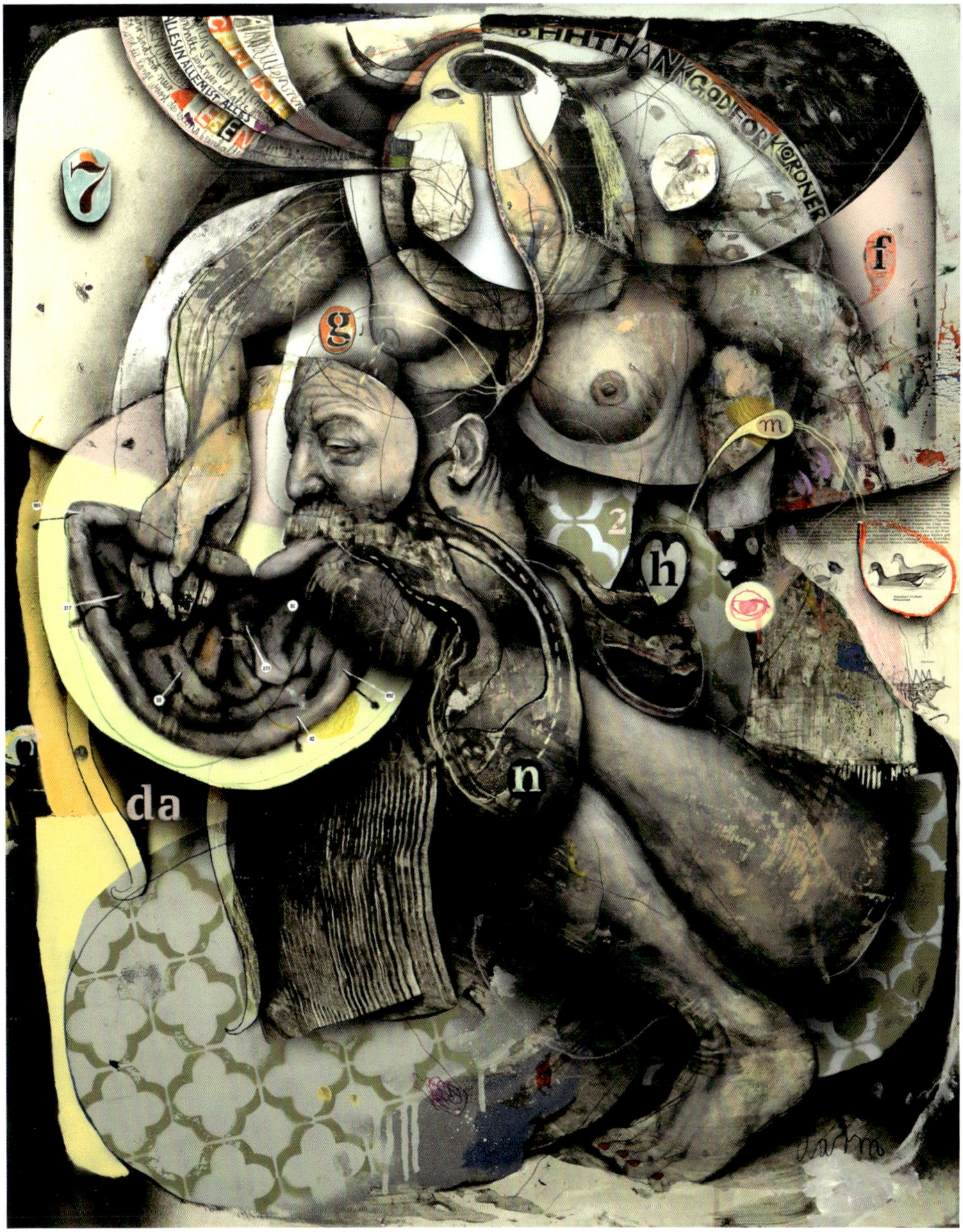

THANKGODFORKRONER
7
f
g
m
2
h
n
da

sitzgeschäftling, ein gasbläser | sitting businesser (a gasblower)

2020, Mixed Media on Canvas, 180 x 150 cm

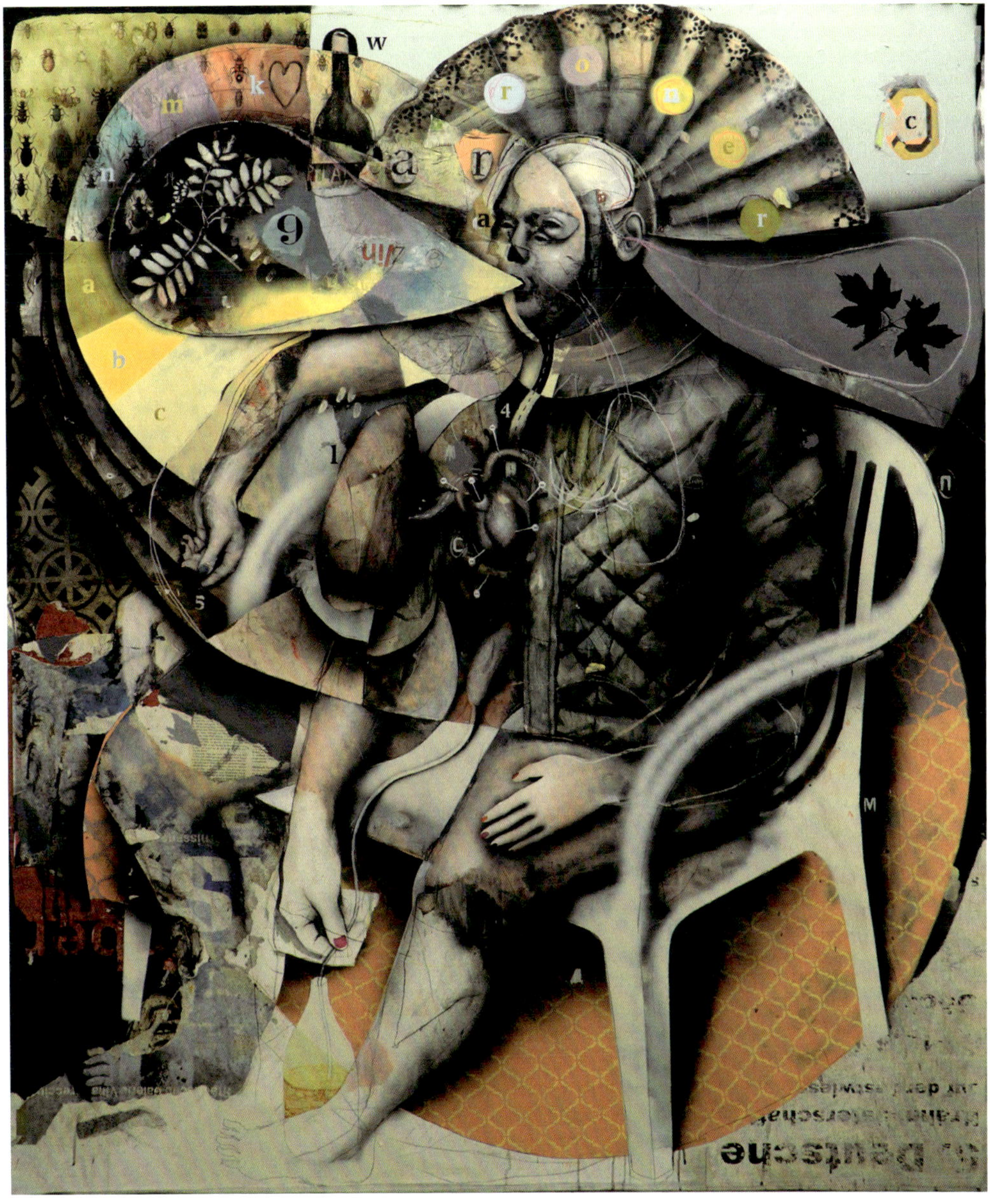

bienenkönig | king bee

2020, Mixed Media on Canvas, 250 x 170 cm
Privatsammlung Deutschland | Private Collection Germany

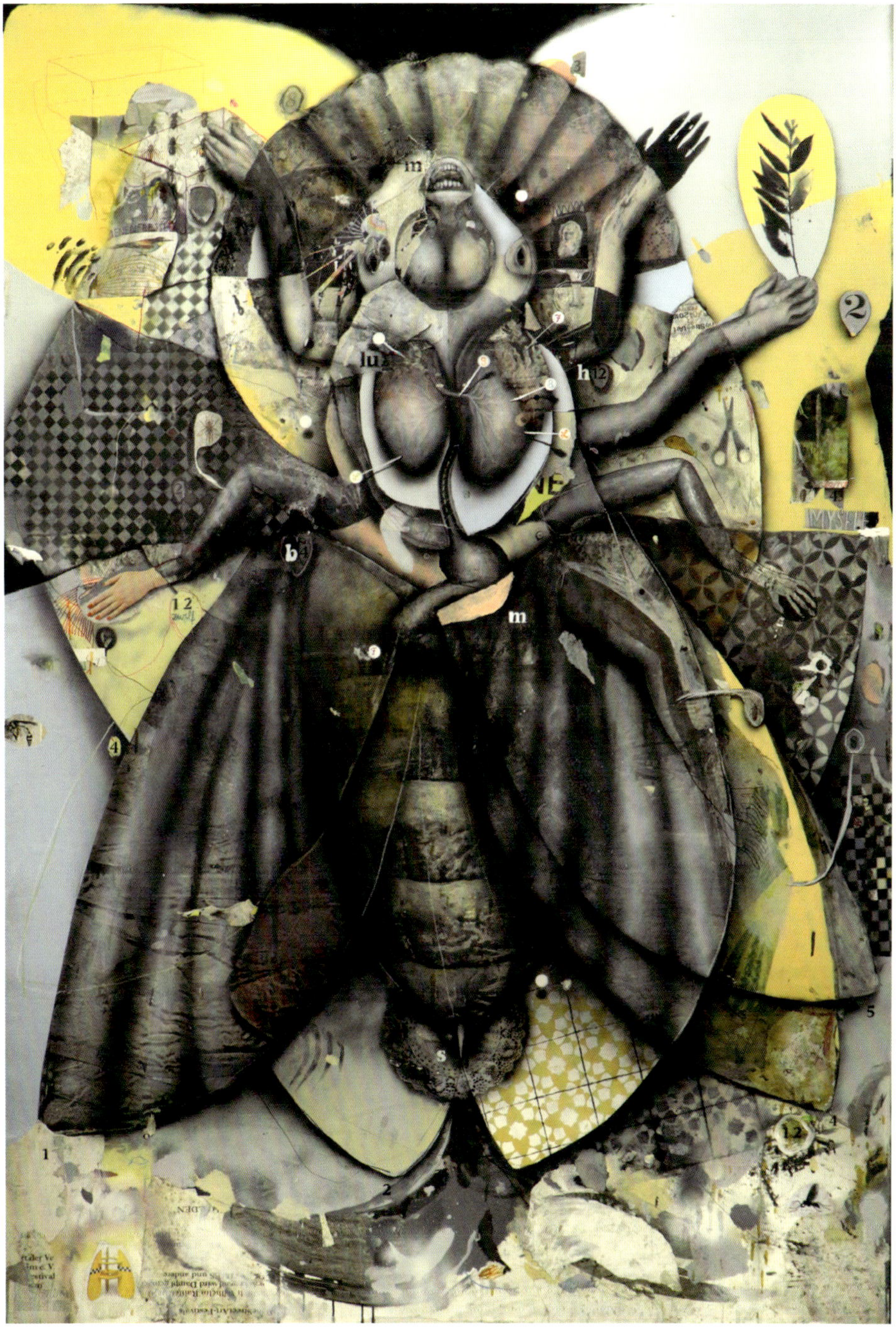

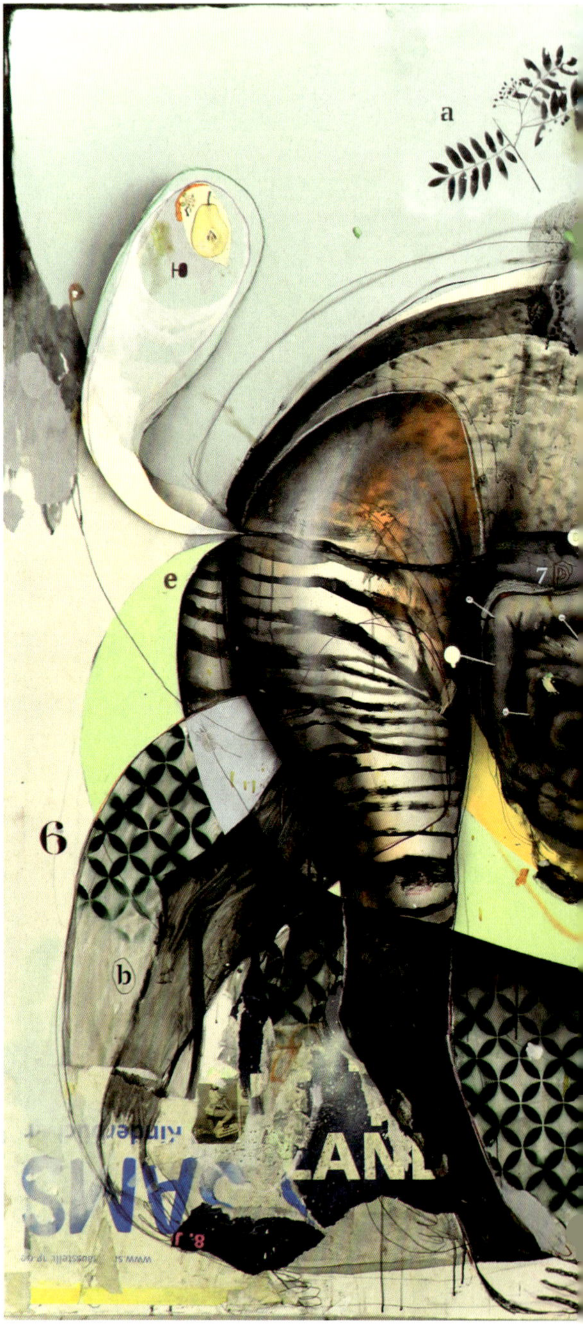

okkuppi (grenzüberritt des grenzüberreiters)
occuppy (border crossing ride of the border crossing rider)

2020, Mixed Media on Canvas, 180 x 250 cm
Privatsammlung Deutschland | Private Collection Germany

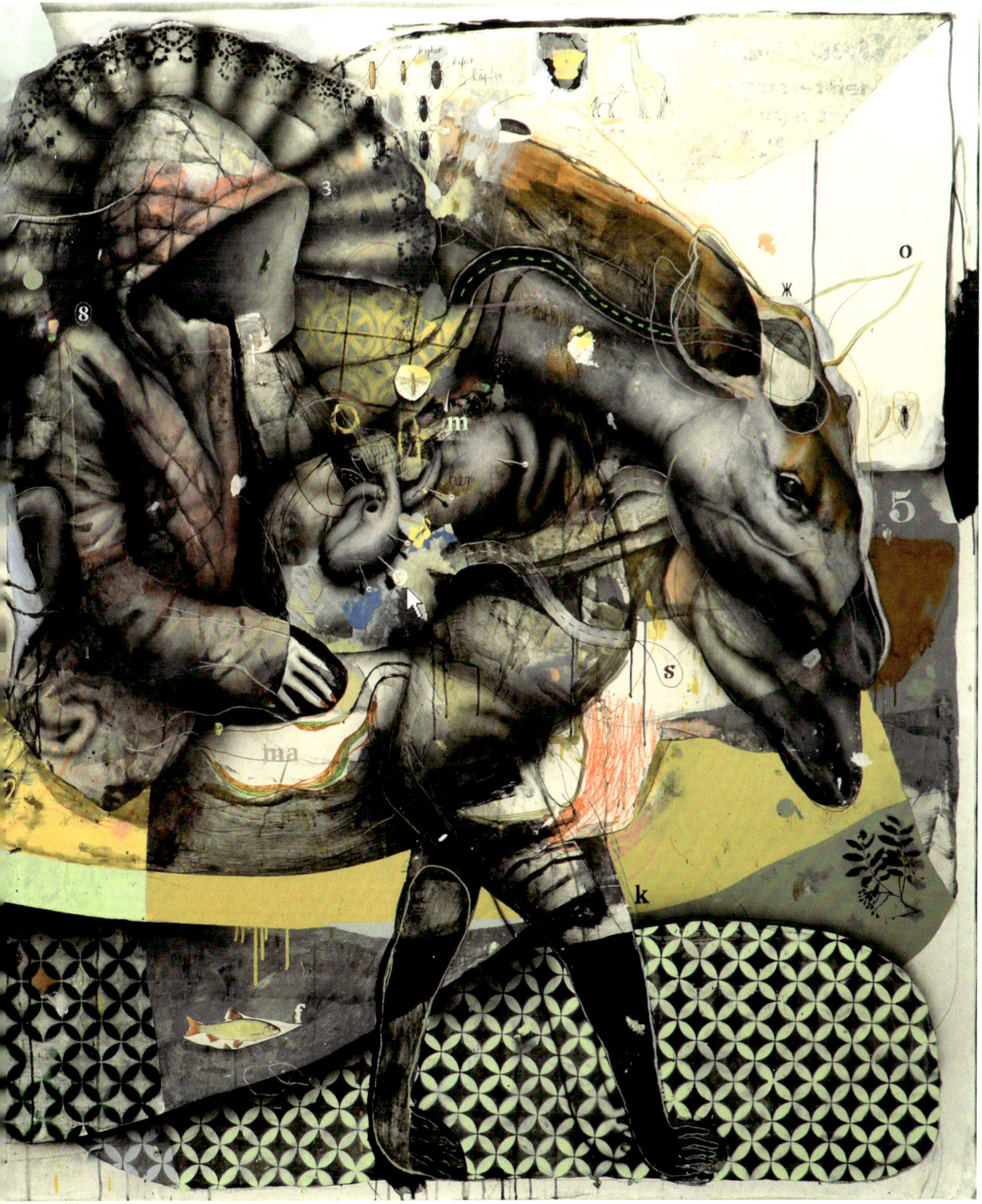
3
8
m
her
5
o
ж
s
ma
k
f

adam und edamer | adam and edamer

2020, Mixed Media on Canvas, 250 x 200 cm

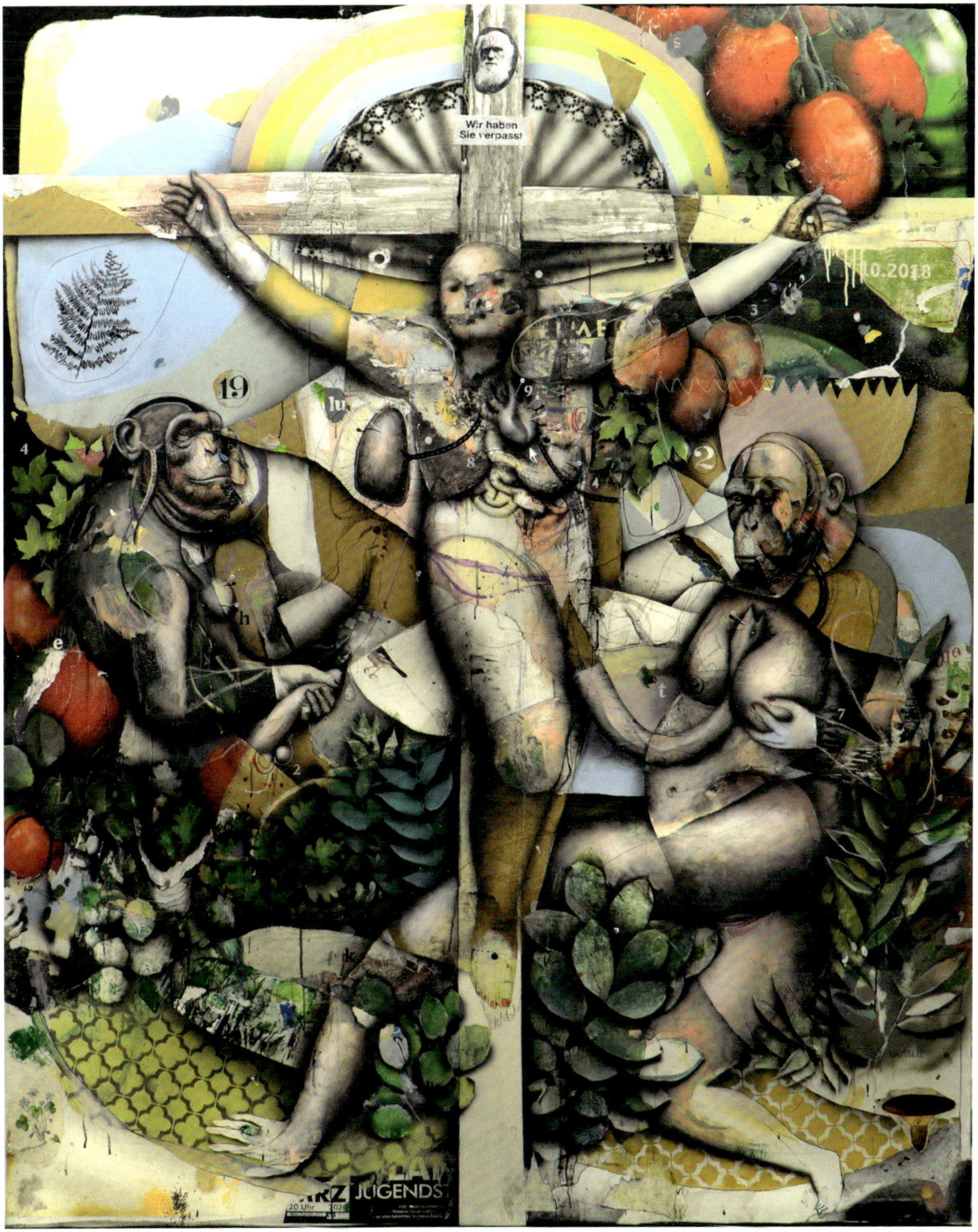
Wir haben
Sie verpasst
10.2018
19
JUGENDS

tante mit bauchladen | aunt with hawker's tray

2020, Mixed Media on Canvas, 150 x 70 cm
Privatsammlung Deutschland | Private Collection Germany

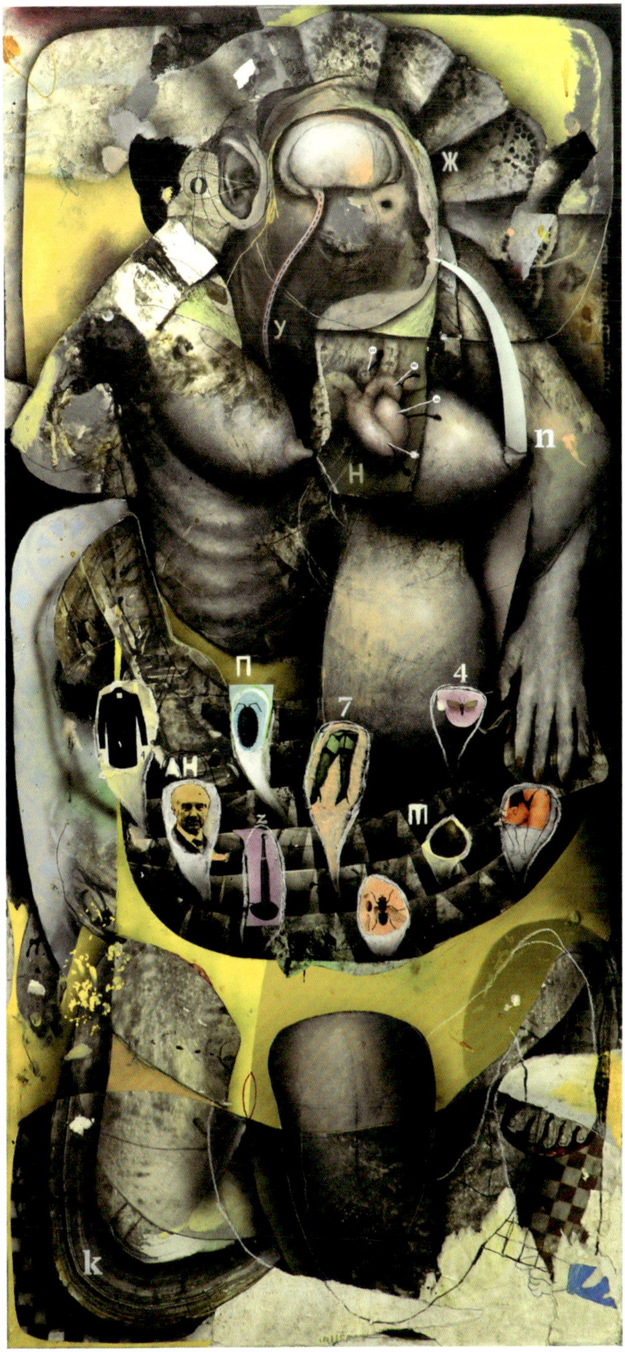
о
ж
у
n
Н
П
4
7
АН
Ш
k

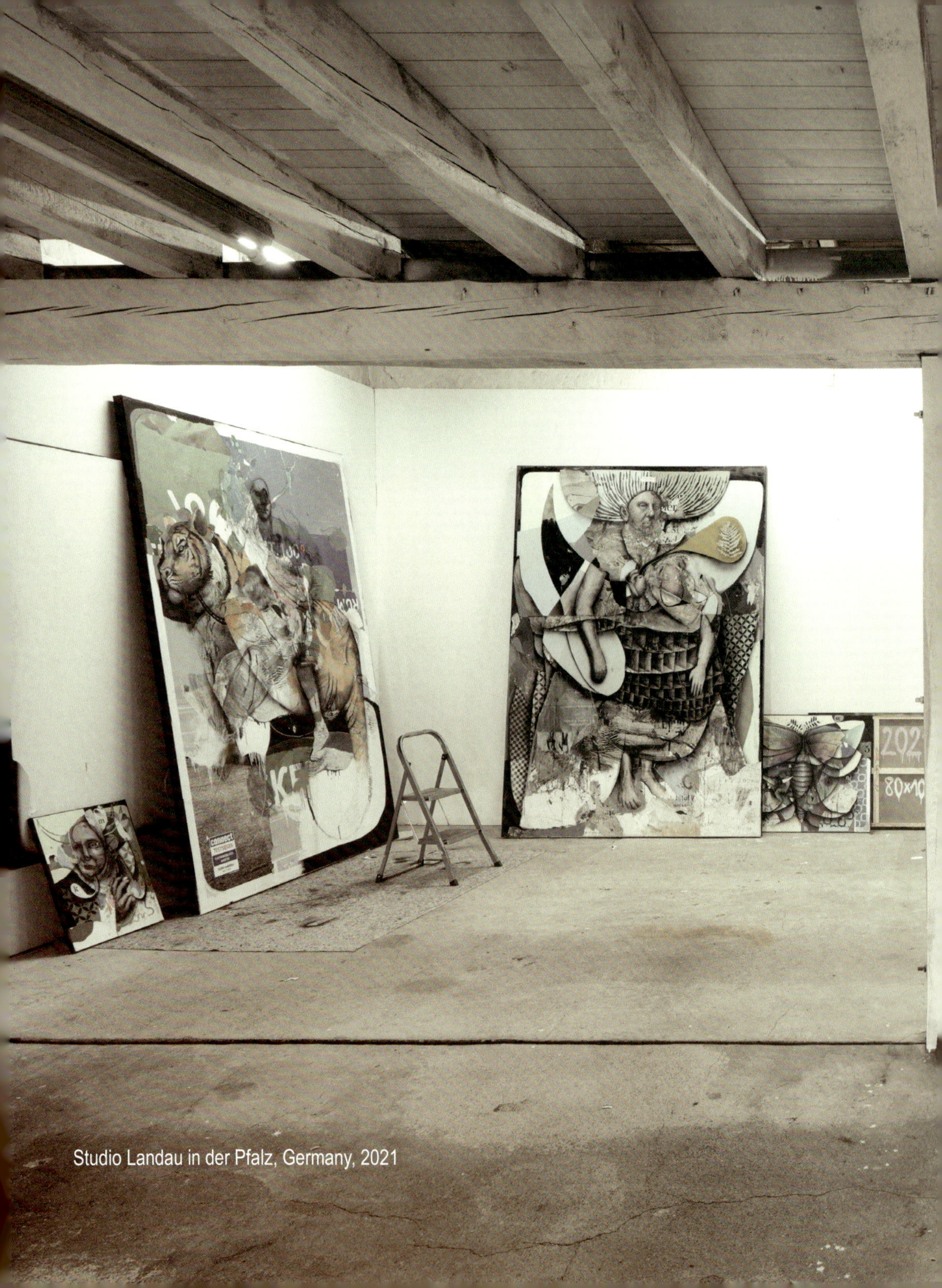

Studio Landau in der Pfalz, Germany, 2021

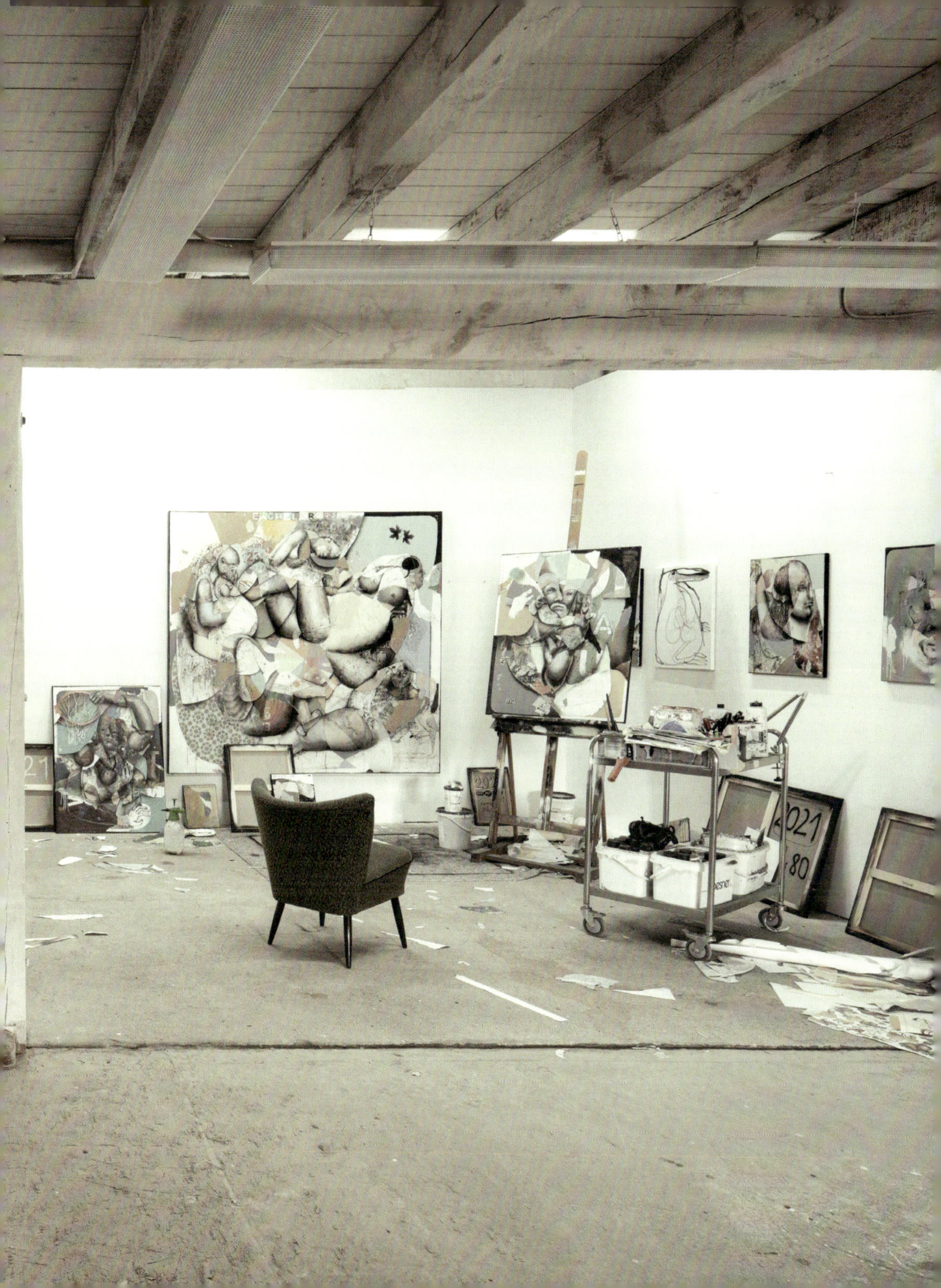
2021
80

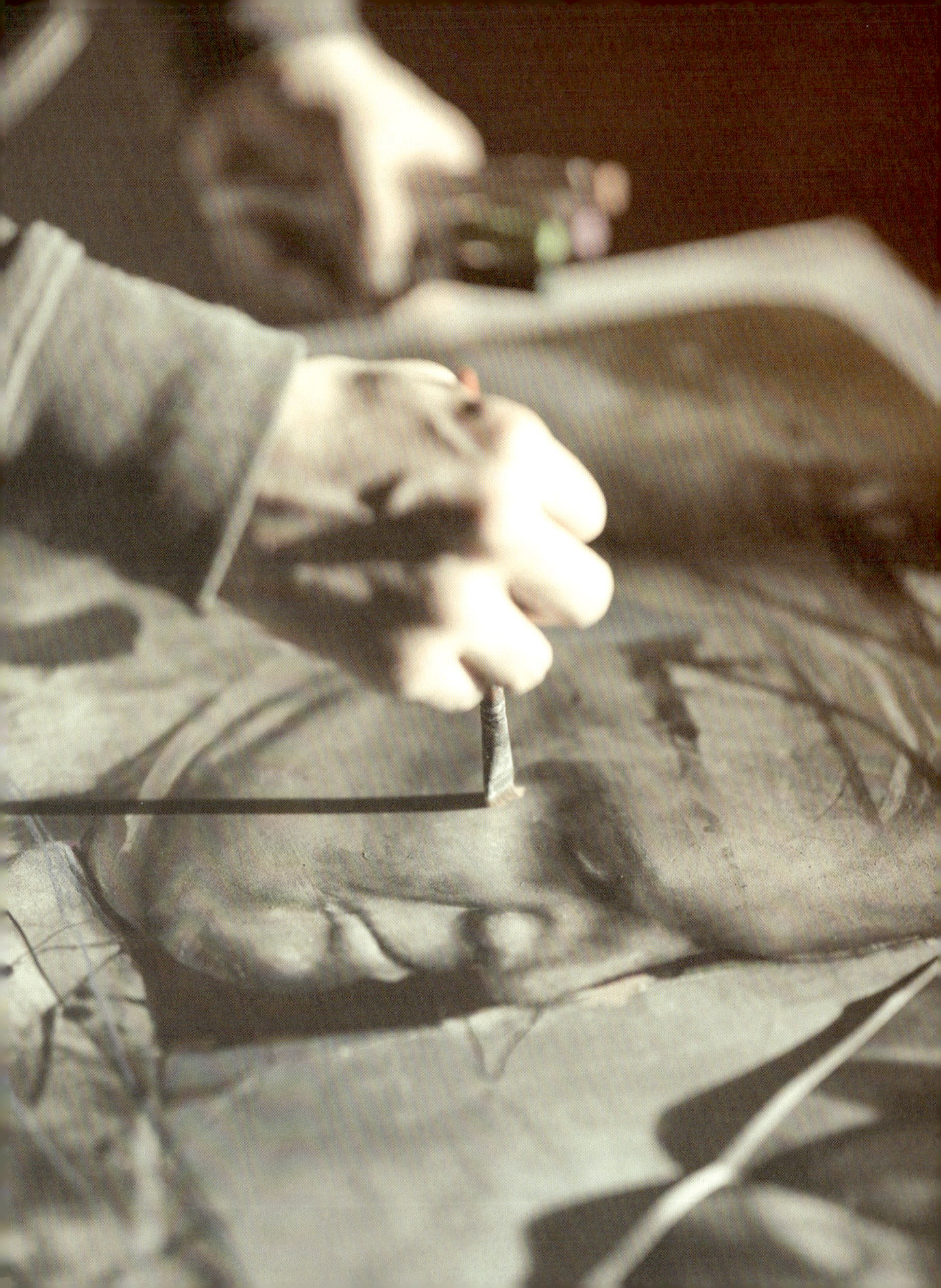

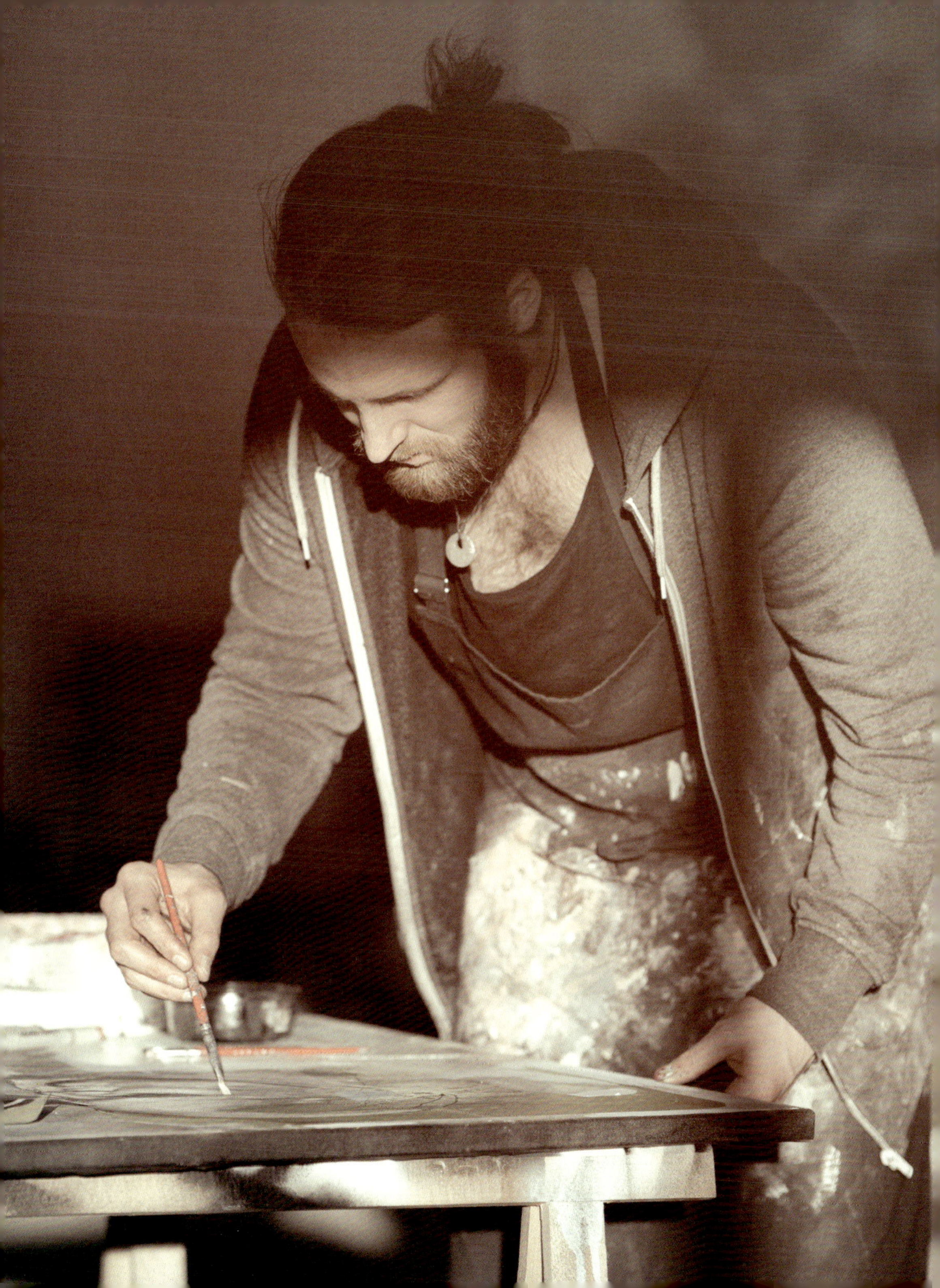

ein geweih wär mir lieber gewesen | I would have preferred an antler

2021, Mixed Media on Canvas, 60 x 50 cm

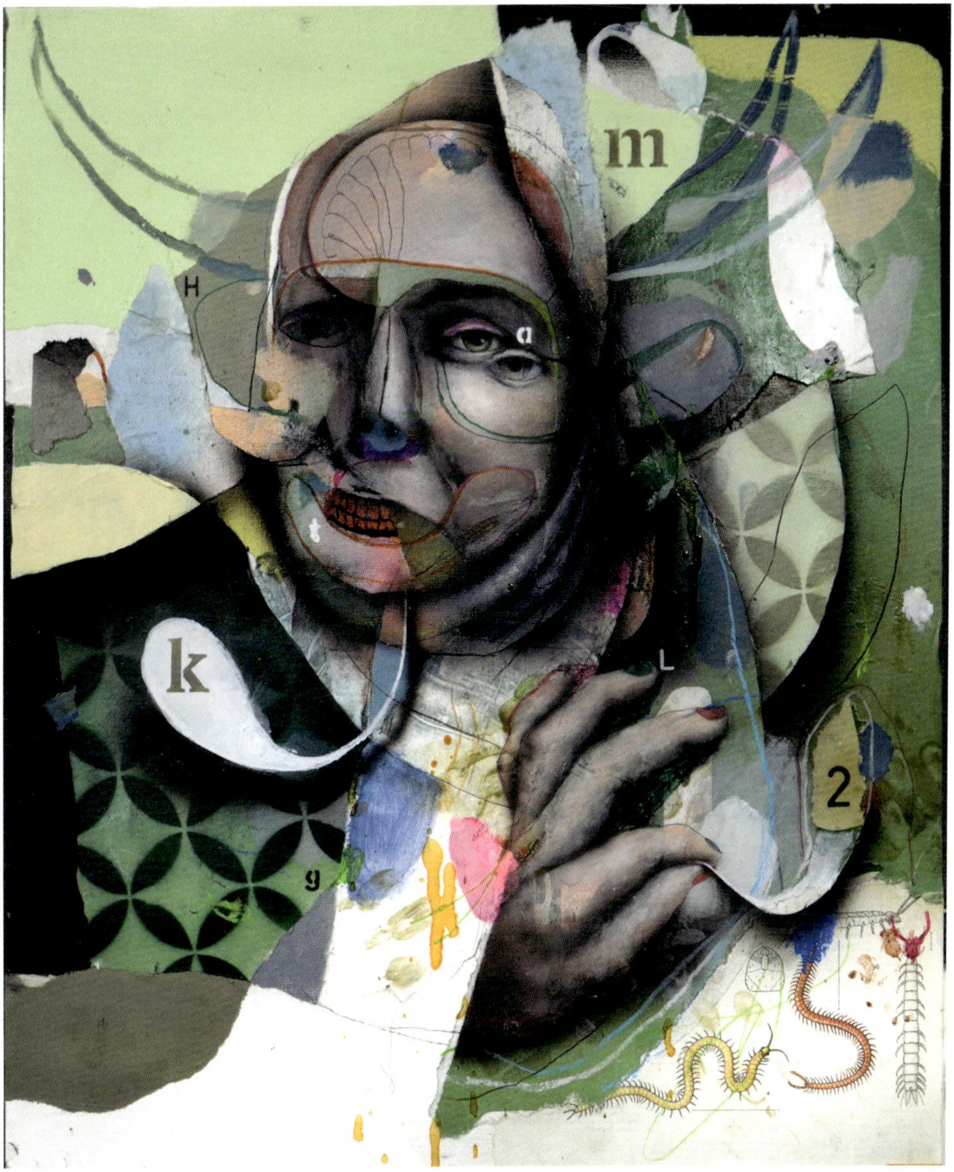

mietzmuffel | kitty pooper

2021, Mixed Media on Canvas, 60 x 50 cm

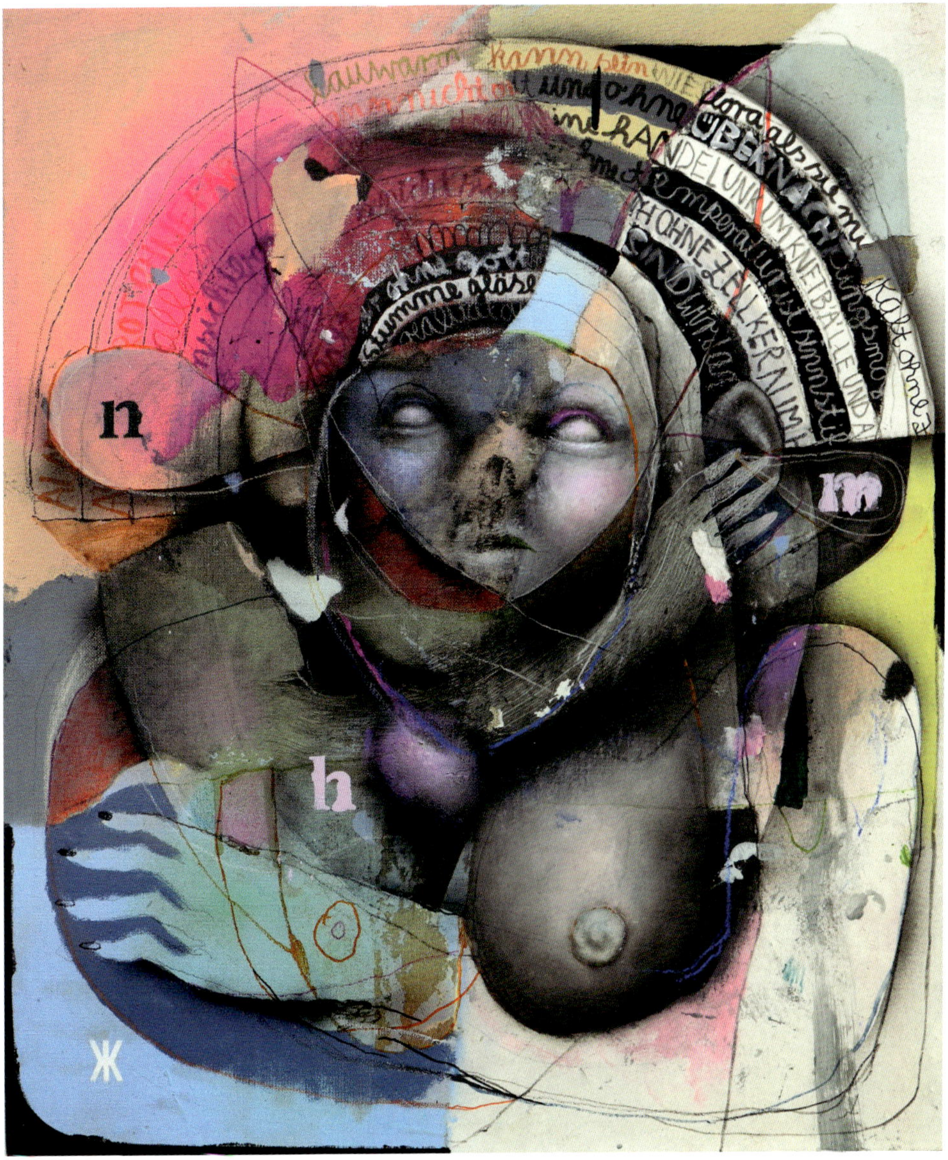
n
ohne gott
stumme gläser
m
h

hund und zunge | dog and tongue

2021, Mixed Media on Canvas, 60 x 50 cm

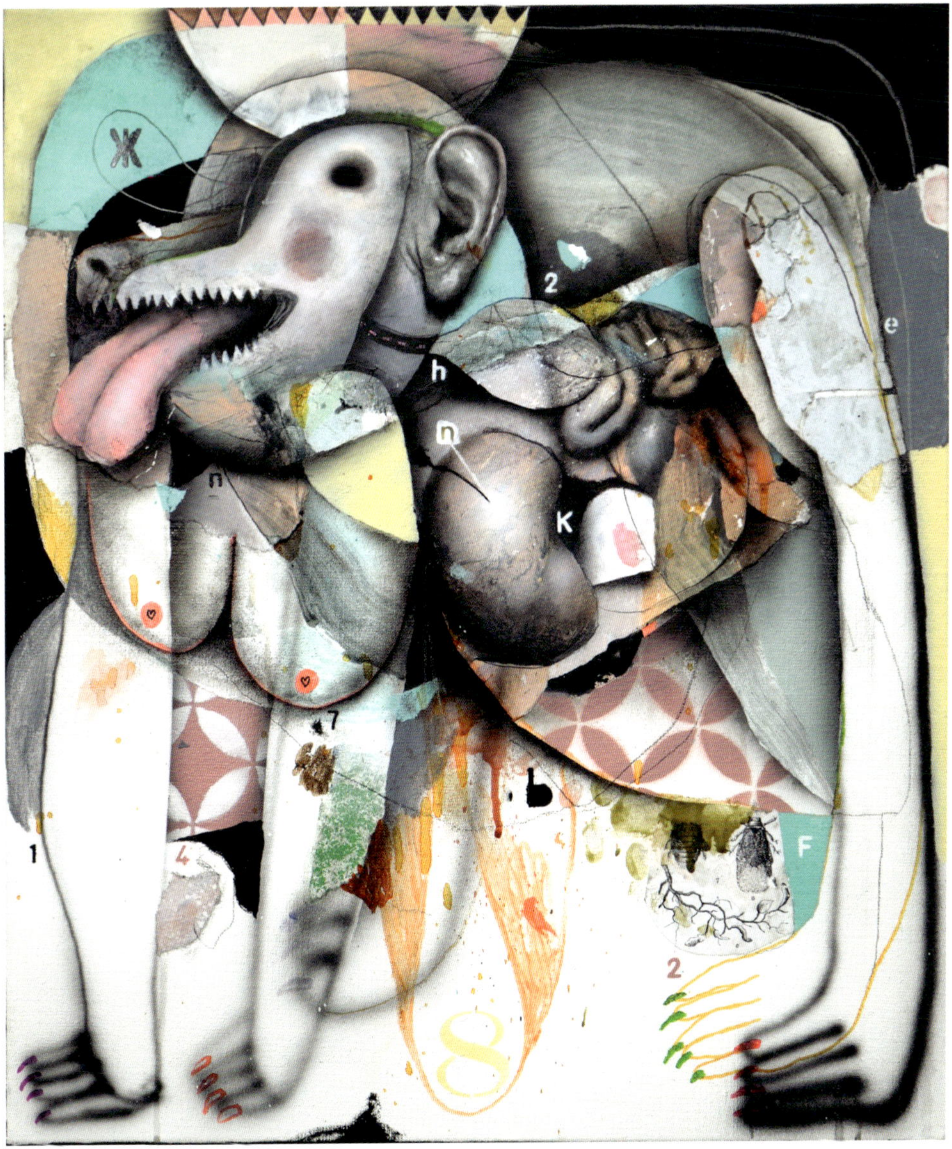

2
e
h
n
n
K
7
1
4
F
2
8

hormonbohrer (happy hypo) | hormone driller (happy hypo)

2021, Mixed Media on Canvas, 60 x 50 cm
Privatsammlung Deutschland | Private Collection Germany

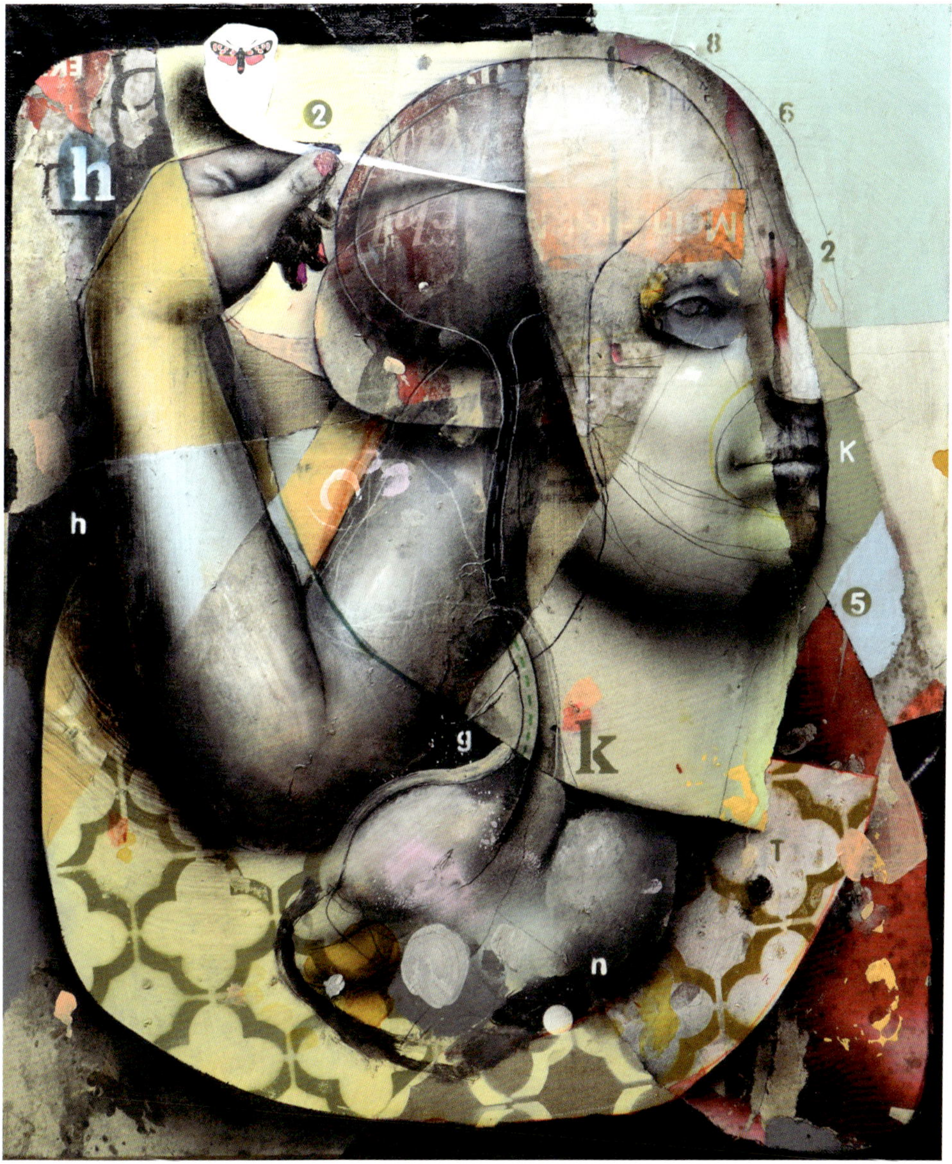

air lambrecht

2021, Mixed Media on Canvas, 100 x 80 cm

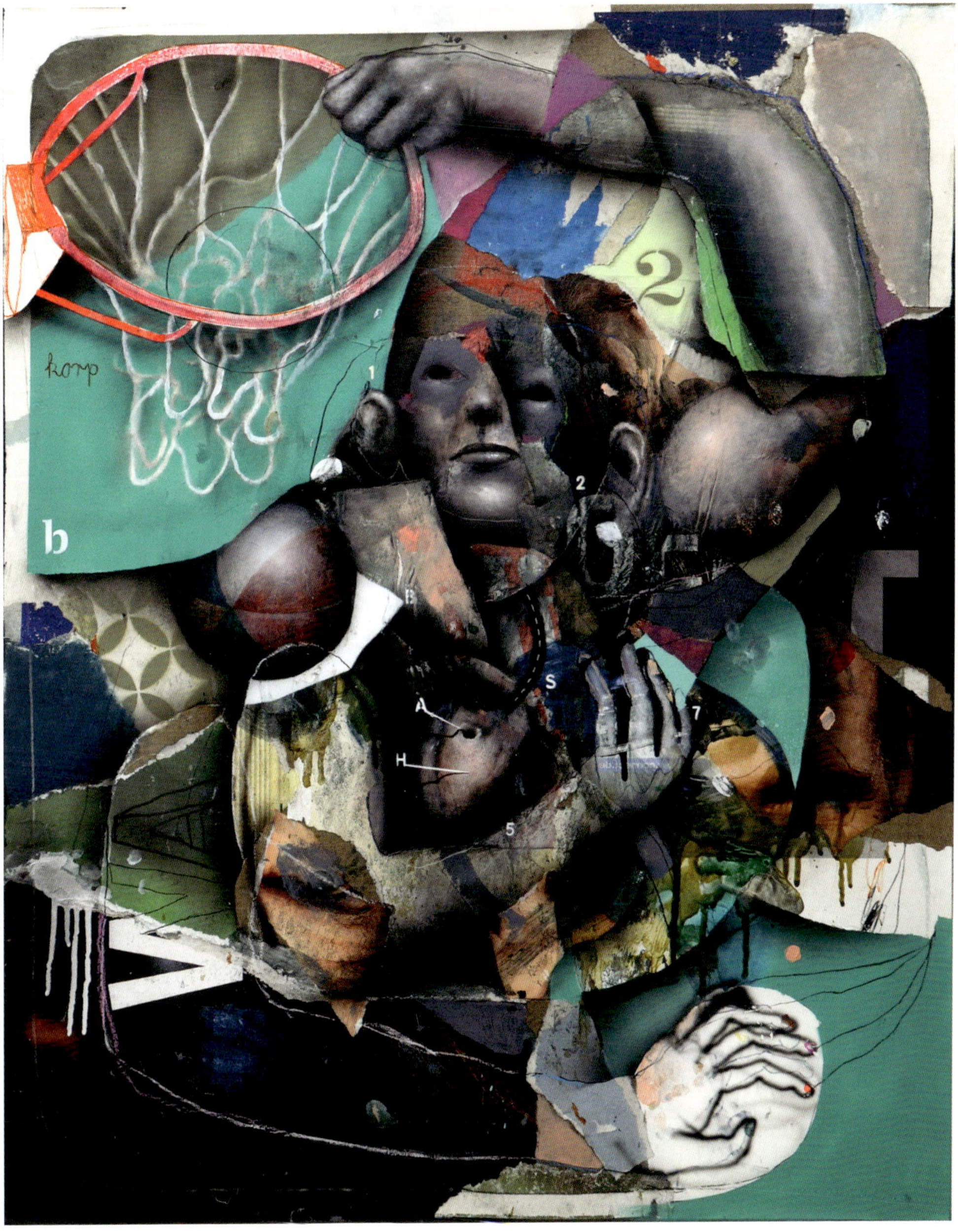
korp
b
2
1
2
A
H
S
7
5

großer ohrenstäbler (ganztags) | the great q-tipper (full-time)

2021, Mixed Media on Canvas, 100 x 80 cm

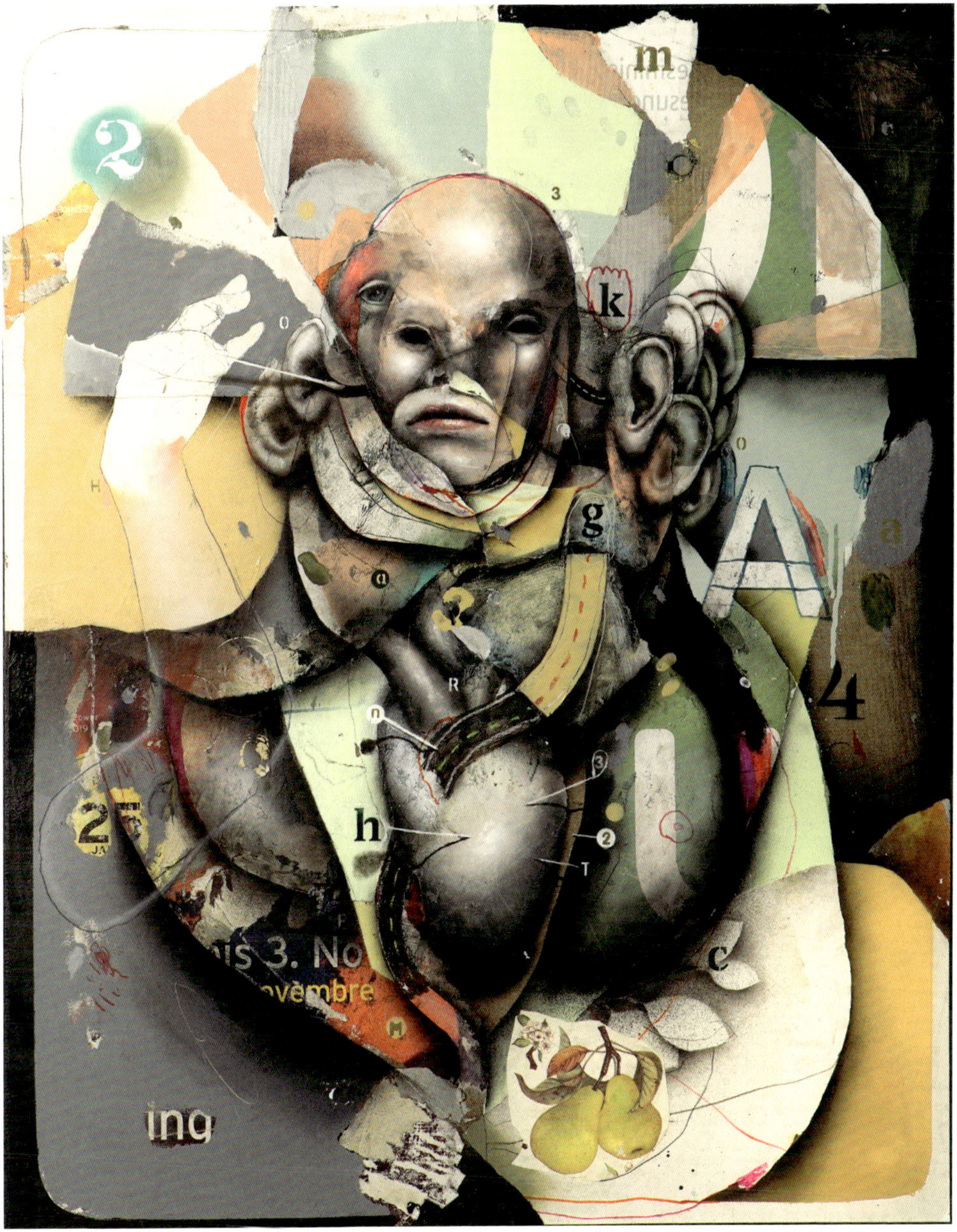
m
2
k
g
A
4
h
is 3. No
ovembre
ing

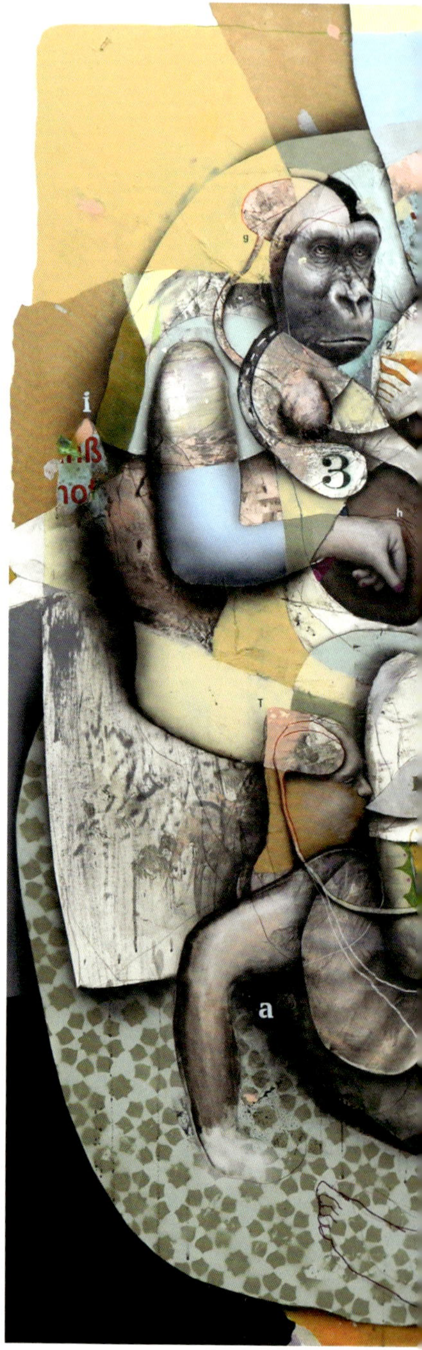

eichelkreis | glans circle

2021, Mixed Media on Canvas, 180 x 200 cm

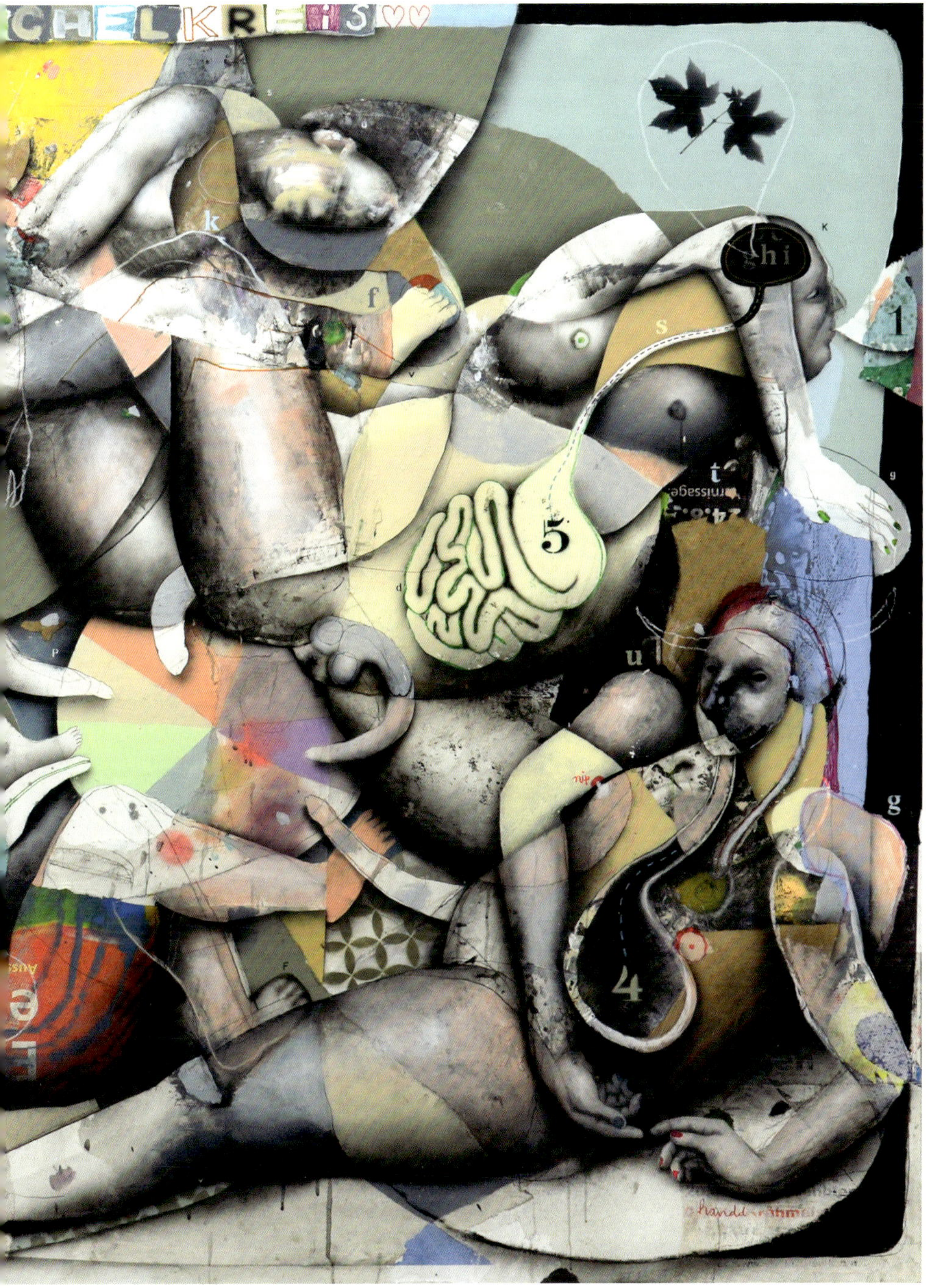
CHELKREiS

schlafradler | sleeping cyclist

2021, Mixed Media on Canvas, 180 x 150 cm

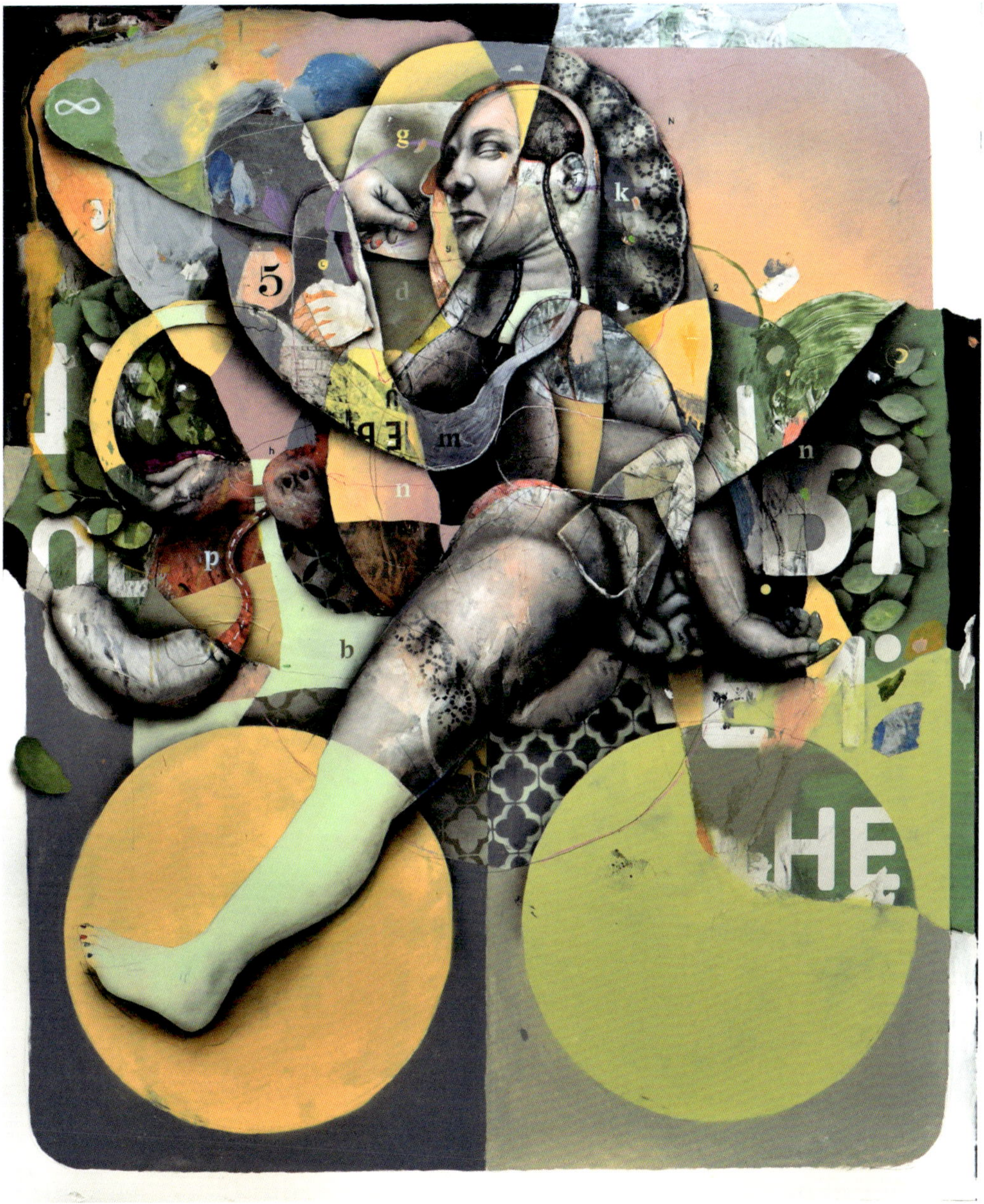

nudelsiebtheoretiker | noodle colander theorist

2021, Mixed Media on Canvas, 250 x 180 cm

Nächste Seite / Next Page

Groupshow, »BALSAM«,
Galerie Thomas Hühsam, Offenbach am Main, Germany, 2021

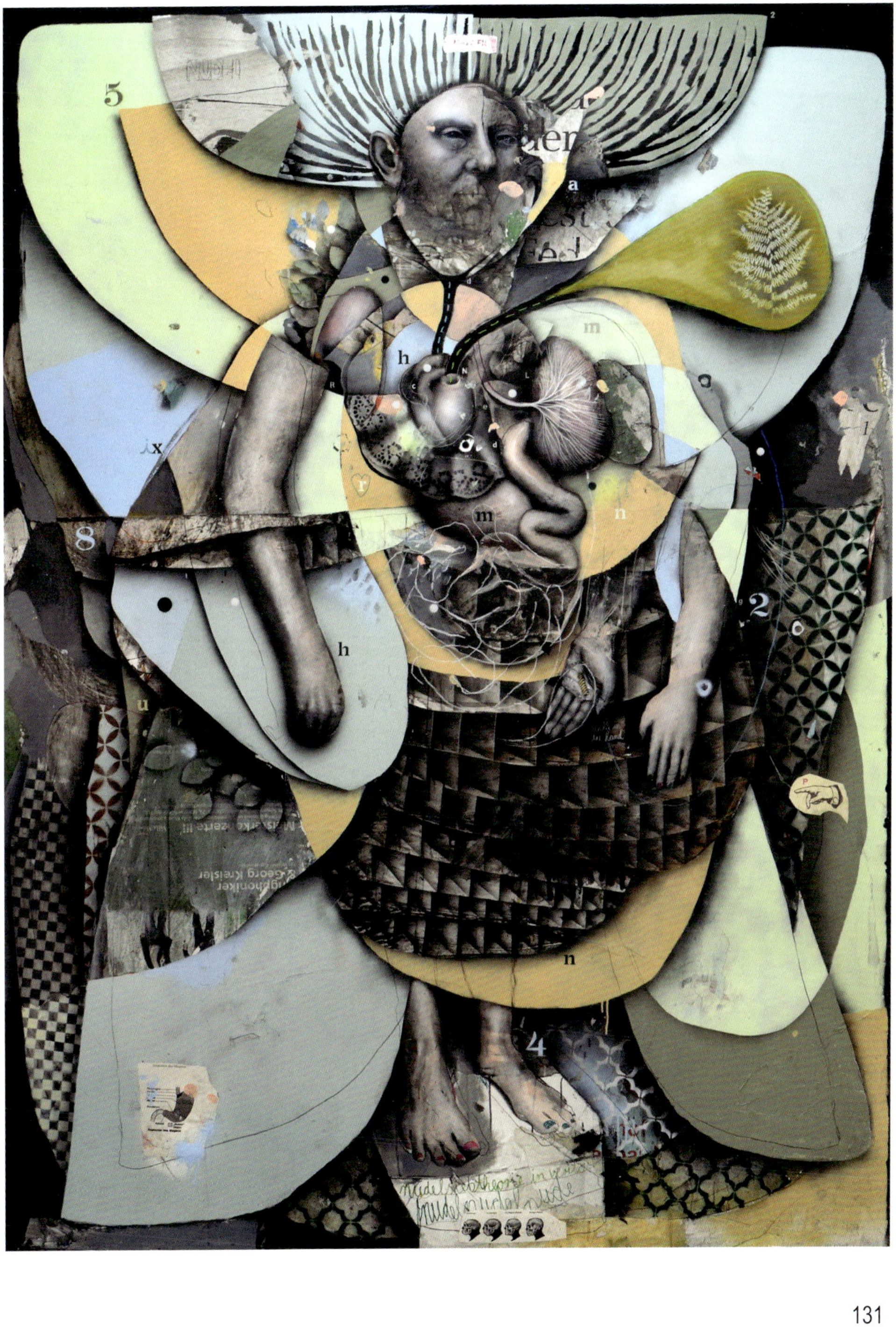

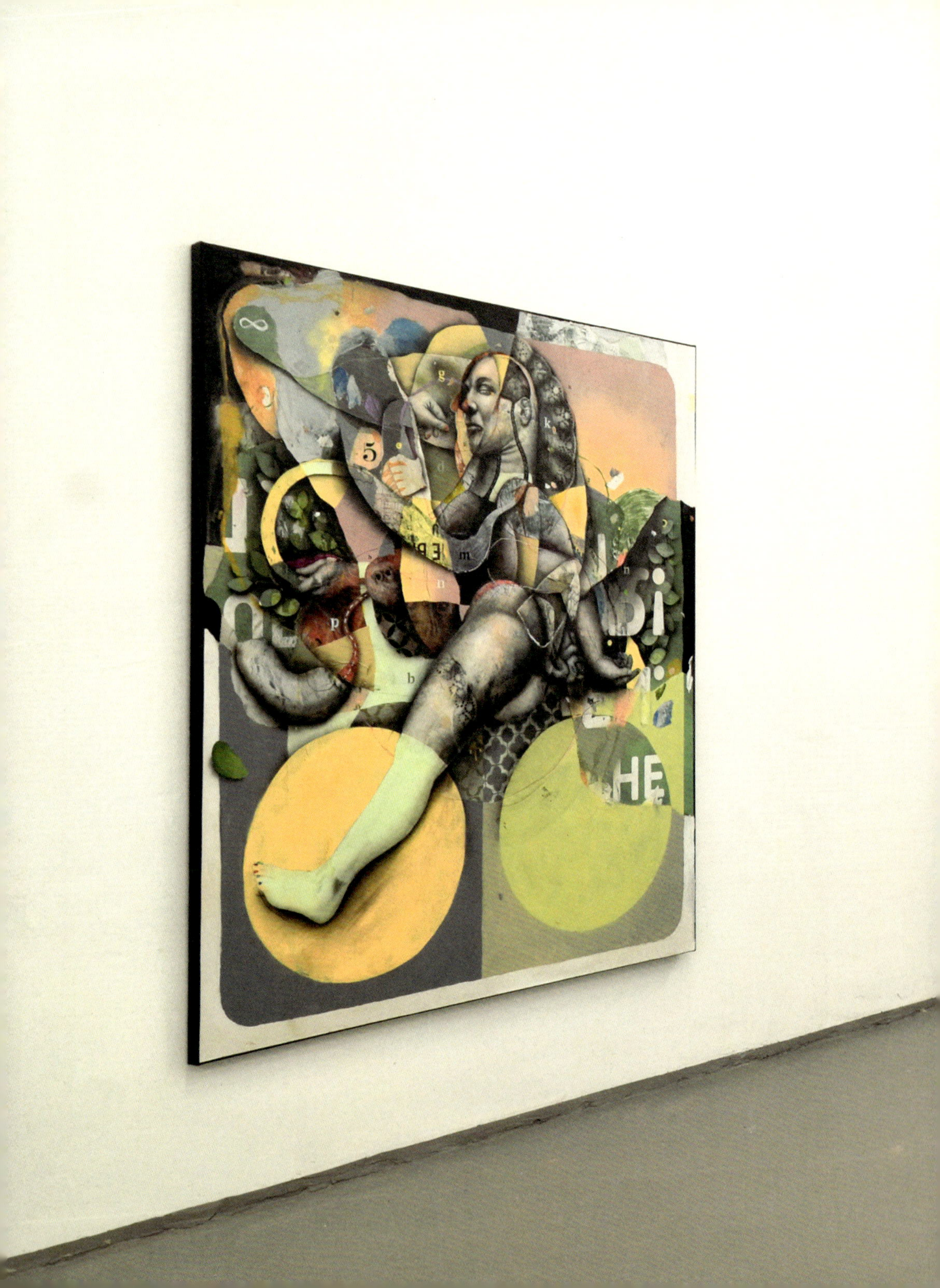

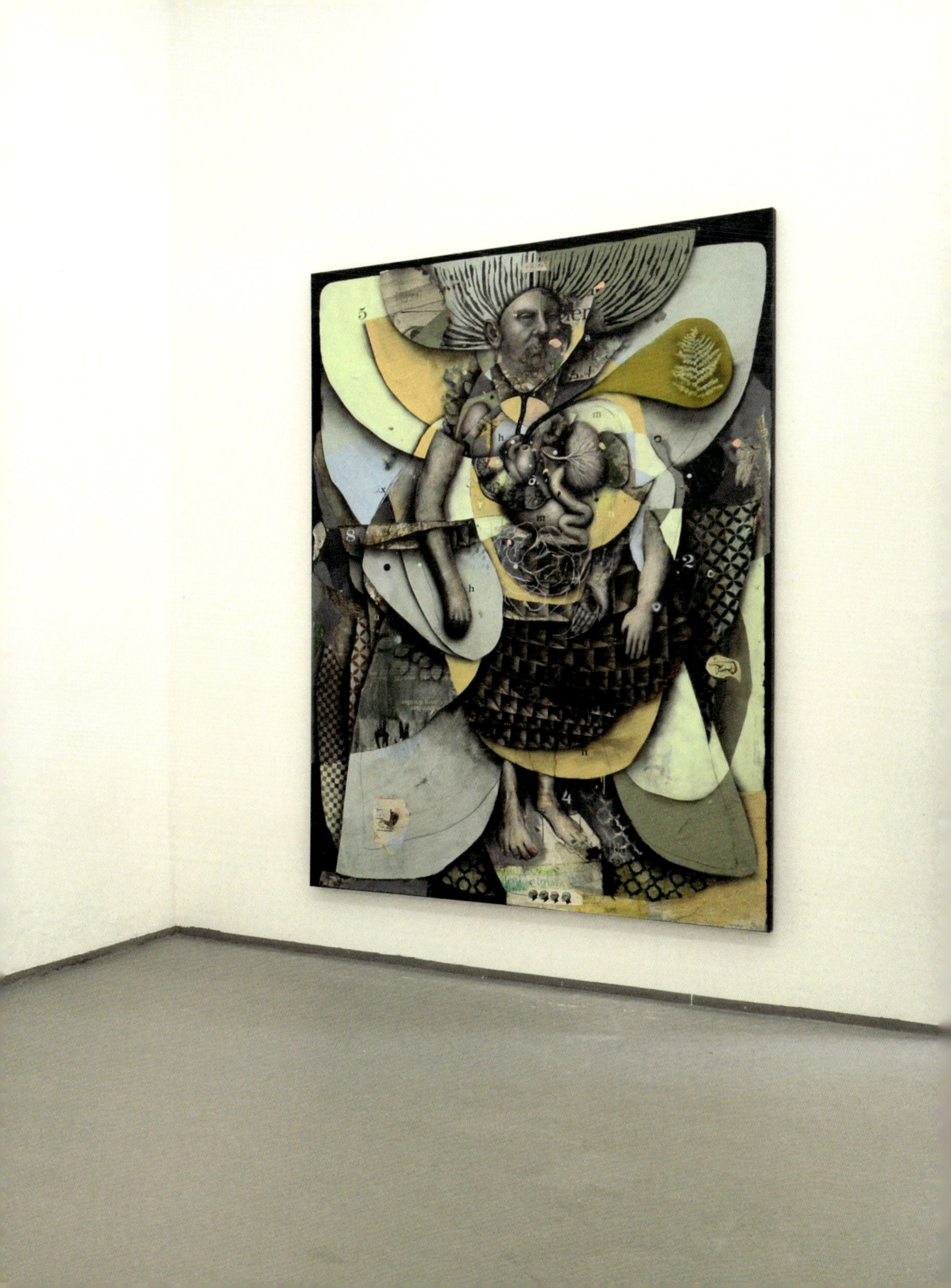

Dominik Schmitt
Biografie | Biography

1983 geboren in Neustadt an der Weinstraße | born in Neustadt an der Weinstraße, Germany

2005 Universität Koblenz-Landau, Campus Landau | University of Koblenz-Landau, Campus Landau, Germany
Studium bei Günther Berlejung | Student of Günther Berlejung

2015 Abschluss: Master of Education | Degree: Master's in Education

2016 Freischaffend | Freelance
lebt und arbeitet in Landau in der Pfalz | lives and works in Landau in der Pfalz, Germany

Einzelausstellungen (Auswahl) | Solo shows (Selection)

2021 Wien (AT), Galerie Felix Höller
Connecticut (USA), The CAMP Gallery

2020 Offenbach am Main (Ger), Galerie Thomas Hühsam, »status quo vadis in veritas ananas«
Wien (AT), Galerie Felix Höller »im betrachter des auges«

2019 Wien (AT), Galerie Felix Höller, »sirius«
Karlsruhe (Ger), Galerie ARTLETstudio, »Insideout«
Biel (CH), Galerie 95, »fragenzirkus«

2018 Wien (AT), Galerie Felix Höller, »anatomie der vernunft«
Offenbach am Main (Ger), Galerie Thomas Hühsam, »kausalkanon«

2017 Wien (AT), Galerie Felix Höller, »ad absurdum«
Landau in der Pfalz (Ger), Galerie M am Deutschen Tor

2015 Frankenthal (Ger), Kunsthaus, »dunkelbunt«
Bad Bergzabern (Ger), Artgalerie, Südpfälzische Kunstgilde e. V., »KRIEG«
Rockenhausen (Ger), Museum Kahnweilerhaus, »KRIEG«

2012 Jena (Ger), Galerie Kunsthof, »selbstgeburt«
Neustadt an der Weinstraße (Ger), Villa Böhm, Kunstverein Neustadt an der Weinstraße e. V., »selbstgeburt«
Mannheim (Ger), Alte Feuerwache, »Lange Nacht der Museen«

2010 Wörth am Rhein (Ger), Haus der Künstler, Heinrich-von-Zügel-Stipendium
Viernheim (Ger), Humboldt Galerie

Gruppenausstellungen, Messen (Auswahl) | Group shows, Art fairs (Selection)

2021 Hamburg (Ger), Galerie B, »Opening«
New York (USA), Spring Break Art Show, The CAMP Gallery
Offenbach am Main (Ger), Galerie Thomas Hühsam, »Balsam«
Seewalchen (AT), Galerie Felix Höller am Attersee, »Best of«
Offenbach am Main (Ger), Galerie Thomas Hühsam, »Mit Kunst infiziert II«

2020 Southampton (USA), Hamptons Art Fair, The CAMP Gallery
Seewalchen (AT), Galerie Felix Höller am Attersee, »Sommerausstellung Galerie Felix Höller«
Offenbach am Main (Ger), Galerie Thomas Hühsam, »Mit Kunst infiziert«
Bad Soden (Ger), Stadtgalerie, »Garten Eden - Künstler blicken ins Paradies«
Offenbach am Main (Ger), Kunstverein Offenbach am Main, »Sammlung Karminsky«
München (Ger), Galerie Benjamin Eck, »Naima Aouni & Dominik Schmitt«
Köln (Ger), Discovery Art Fair.Virtual, Galerie Felix Höller

2019 New York (USA), SCOPE Art Show, The Directed Art Modern
Miami (USA), The Directed Art Modern
Münster (Ger), Galerie ARTLETstudio, »Surreal Positions«
Frankfurt (Ger), Discovery Art Fair, Galerie Thomas Hühsam
Neustadt an der Weinstraße (Ger), Villa Böhm, »For Your Eyes Only«

2018 Basel (CH), SCOPE Art Show, janinebeangallery
Palm Beach (USA), Art Palm Beach, The Directed Art Modern
Berlin (Ger), janinebeangallery, »Strange Matter«
Częstochowa (PL), Miejska Galeria Sztuki, »INCIDENT ACCIDENT«
Berlin (Ger), Museum für Moderne Kunst, Berlinische Galerie | Museum of Modern Art
Wien (AT), Galerie Felix Höller
Münster (Ger), Galerie ARTLETstudio, »a symbolic summer«

2017 Berlin (Ger), Museum für moderne Kunst, Berlinische Galerie | Museum of Modern Art
Basel (CH), SCOPE Art Show, janinebeangallery
Berlin (Ger), mianki.gallery
Büdelsdorf (Ger), NordArt 2017
Berlin (Ger), janinebeangallery, »Dominik Schmitt & Daniel Harms«
Karlsruhe (Ger), Galerie ARTLETstudio, »Begegnungen«
Paris (F), Maison Européenne de la Photographie, »ARTE Video Night« | Center for contemporary photographic art
München (Ger), ARTMUC, Internationale Messe für zeitgenössische Kunst | International Art Fair for Contemporary Art
Magdeburg (Ger), KunstMitte, Mitteldeutsche Messe für zeitgenössische Kunst | Art Fair for Contemporary Art
Ludwigshafen (Ger), Kunstverein Ludwigshafen, »Emy Roeder Preis 2017«

2016 Miami Beach (USA), Art Basel Week, Savoy, »DAM ART 2016«
Offenbach am Main (Ger), Galerie Thomas Hühsam, »Schwindelsicht«
Köln (Ger), Galerie Luzia Sassen, »von Punkt zu Punkt«
Essen (Ger), Contemporary Art Ruhr, Messe für zeitgenössische Kunst | Art Fair for Contemporary Art
Wien (A), Palais Kinsky, Ausstellung und Auktion zeitgenössischer Kunst | Exhibition and Auction of Contemporary Art
Neustadt an der Weinstraße-Mußbach (Ger), Kunsthalle Herrenhof, »Vier der Besten aus dem Südwesten«

2015 Wien (A), Palais Kinsky, Ausstellung und Auktion zeitgenössischer Kunst | Exhibition and Auction of Contemporary Art
Paris (F), Maison Européenne de la Photographie, »ARTE Video Night« | Center for contemporary photographic art
Neustadt an der Weinstraße-Mußbach (Ger), Herrenhof, »Der Anker«
Haifa (Isr), Gate 3 Gallery
Paris (F), »FIAC« (Foire internationale d'art contemporain), ARTE creative | International Contemporary Art Fair
Landau in der Pfalz (Ger), Universität Koblenz-Landau, Atelier Lazarettstraße, Absolventenausstellung

Impressum | Colophon

Diese Publikation erscheint anlässlich der Ausstellung | This publication is released to accompany the exhibition
»BALSAM«, Dominik Schmitt & Benjamin Burkard, 15.5. - 17.7.2021, Galerie Thomas Hühsam, Offenbach am Main, Germany

Herausgeber | Editor
Galerie Thomas Hühsam, Offenbach am Main, Germany

Redaktion | Editorial Staff
Thomas Hühsam

Gestaltung | Design
Dominik Schmitt

Lektorat | Copyediting
Helen Roth, Neil Solomon

Übersetzungen | Translations
Neil Solomon

Projektmanagement | Project Management, Kerber Verlag
Lydia Fuchs

Herstellung | Production, Kerber Verlag
Jens Bartneck

Fotografien | Photographs
Joshua Mack (Abb. S. 20 - 21), Annemone Taake (Abb. S, 6, 10 - 12, 137), Dominik Schmitt, Jan Robert Weist (Abb. S. 110 - 113)

Gedruckt mit freundlicher Unterstützung von | Published with the kind support of
Galerie Thomas Hühsam, Offenbach am Main; NEUSTART; Ministerium für Kultur und Medien

Gesamtherstellung und Vertrieb | Printed and published by
Kerber Verlag
Windelsbleicher Str. 166 - 170
33659 Bielefeld
Germany
+49 521 950 08 10
+49 521 950 08 88 (F)
info@kerberverlag com
kerberverlag.com

Kerber Publikationen werden weltweit vertrieben | Kerber publications are distributed worldwide

ACC Art Books
Sandy Lane
Old Martlesham
Woodbridge, IP12 4SD
UK
+44 1394 38 99 50
+44 1394 38 99 99 (F)
accartbooks.com
uksales@accartbooks.com

Artbook | D.A.P.
75 Broad Street, Suite 630
New York, NY 10004
USA
+1 (212) 627 19 99
+1 (212) 627 94 84 (F)
artbook.com
orders@dapinc.com

AVA Verlagsauslieferung AG
Centralweg 16
8910 Affoltern am Albis
Switzerland
+41 44 762 42 50
+41 44 762 42 10 (F)
avainfo@ava.ch

Zeitfracht GmbH
Verlagsauslieferung
kerber-verlag@knv-zeitfracht.de

Die Deutsche Nationalbibliothek verzeichnet diese Publikation in der Deutschen Nationalbibliografie: dnb.de.
The Deutsche Nationalbibliothek lists this publication in the Deutsche Nationalbibliografie: dnb.de.

ISBN 978-3-7356-0784-3
www. kerberverlag com
Printed in Germany

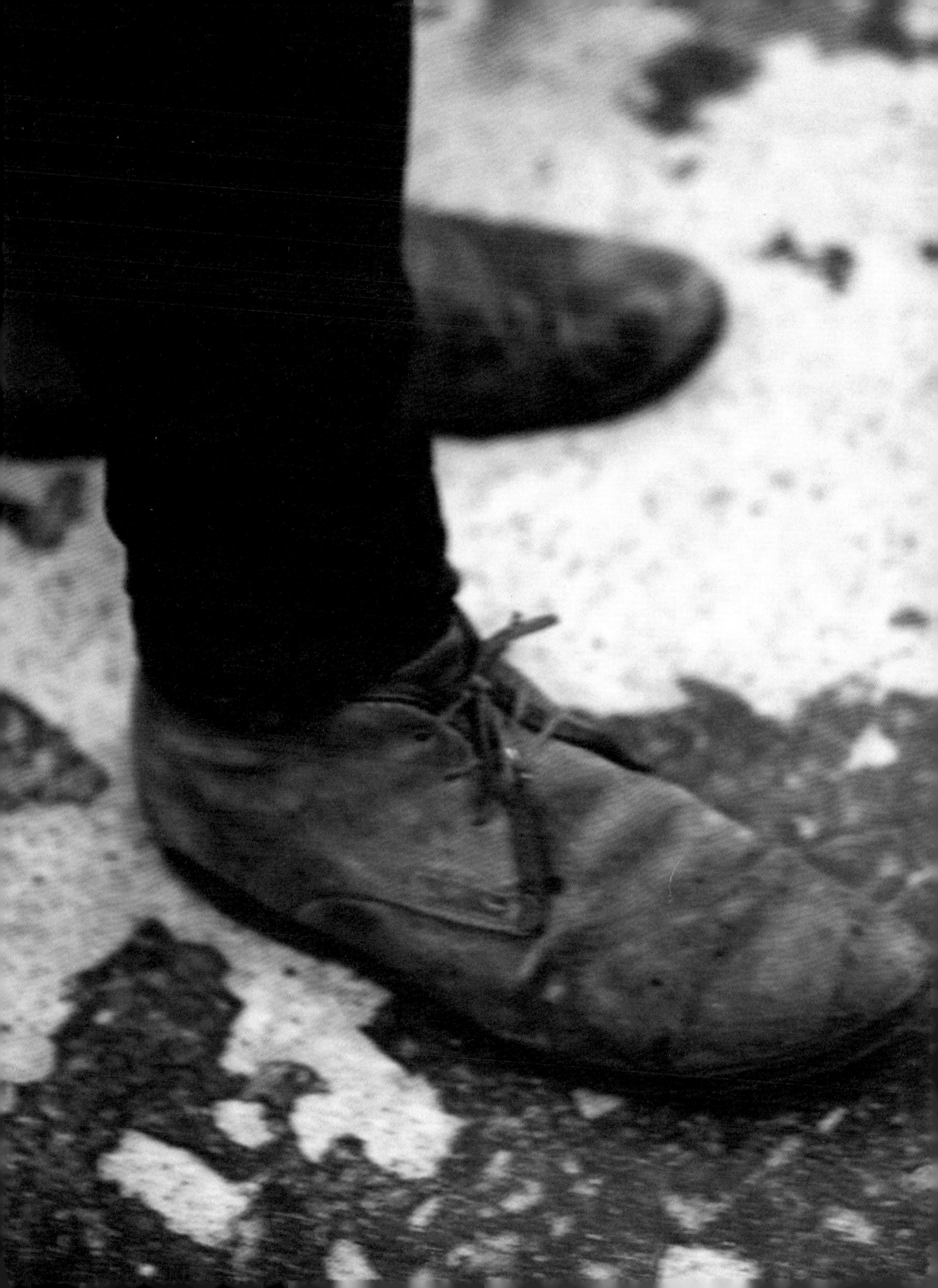

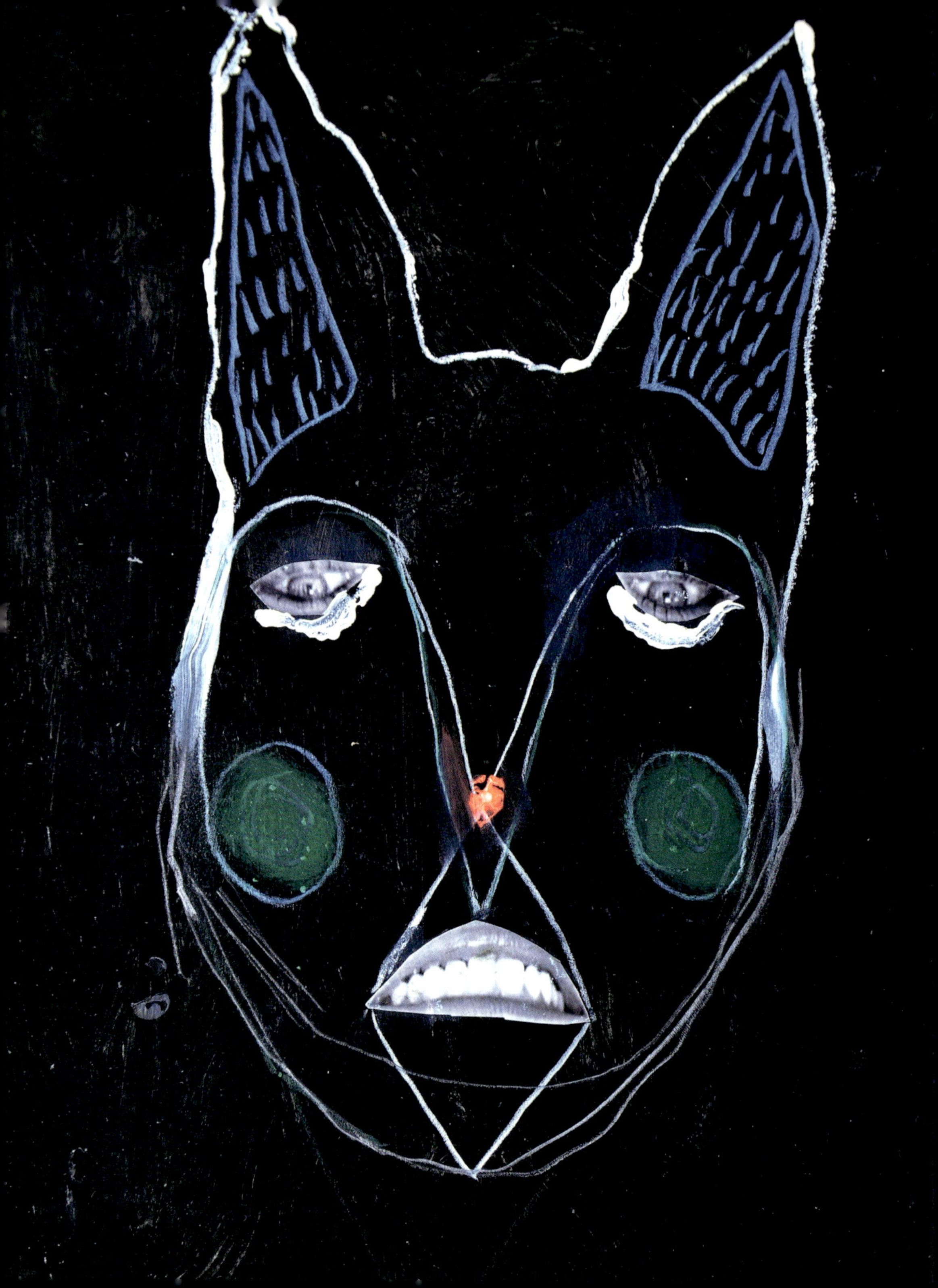